I0797721

Everlasting Blooms

LAYLA ROBINSON

Everlasting Blooms

25+ floristry projects to bring the magic of dried flowers into your life

Contents

Pastels 102

Neutrals 160

Hello

I feel very glad that my flower journey has brought me to where I am today. If you'd asked me when I started growing cut flowers over 15 years ago where I'd be, I couldn't have guessed at all the twists, turns and delights that have unfolded along the way.

As a lover of flowers from a very early age, and with an education in horticulture and garden design, it was an easy decision to start a new business 'Darling Buds of Hay' growing fresh cut flowers in 2009, a year or so after our first daughter was born. In those early days, I made just a few winter wreaths from dried foraged materials in my kitchen, with a lively toddler adding to the chaos. But so the seed of my passion for everlasting flower sculpture was discreetly sown, and gradually grew. This was before everlasting flowers had boomed in popularity, and my work was cut out trying to explain that a wreath was not just for Christmas but could be a beautiful piece of floral art all year round.

I have learned from many mistakes made along the way. For example, storing my entire year's worth of dried hydrangea in bin bags in the shed, only to find they had all gone brown a month later! Over the years, and after having two more daughters, I gained a reputation for my unique, colourful flower sculpture, and made the decision to focus my attention on it entirely.

A life-changing moment came when we built my studio in 2021 and expanded the flower growing area around it. Moving from working in the heart of a hectic family home to having my own warm, light workspace to stretch out in and store my flowers was a game-changer. It enabled my creativity to flourish and new designs to emerge, many of which are in this book.

One breakthrough moment was the invention of the everlasting flower panel, which was inspired by a flower lampshade I made for my daughter Goldie's bedroom a few years ago; I adapted the lampshade design by adding a willow frame to the flat panel and this has now taken off as a new form of floral art around the globe.

After years of experimenting with foraged grasses and flowers, I've come to appreciate how the wild palette can really bring floral art to life. A walk is now full of promise, a foraging adventure every time, always with a pair of scissors in my pocket, my eye-rolling family ever patient as I scamper off (again) to some bramble-filled corner to retrieve a pretty seed head. I am a huge advocate of not only protecting nature and our environment but enhancing and improving it wherever possible. I would love everyone to see floral art as a way of increasing our appreciation of and concern for this abundant world we are so fortunate to gather from.

Through my journey with everlasting flowers, I have been given the chance to work on a wonderful variety of interesting opportunities. Creating stage décor for festivals, TV appearances, art gallery installations, set and photoshoot décor, and working with world-class brands, as well as the joy of teaching others in workshops and my online flower panel tutorial, decorating shops, restaurants and cafés, and keeping up with commissions means you can safely and happily say this life is never boring!

It is an enormous privilege to share my ideas with you in the hope of igniting the spark of creativity that will take you on your own unique and exciting, fun-filled flower adventures. I want to encourage everyone to embrace any mistakes as opportunities, to love being different and to nurture the smallest creative seed within you. From small seeds grow beautiful things, and the excitement is in not knowing quite how they will unfurl. I hope you will be surprised and delighted by what you discover.

Introduction

Within these pages I share the best of my designs; those that I hold close to my heart and have dreamed up after years of experimenting. There can be so much more to dried flower art than the traditional, old-fashioned arrangements of the past (although they can be very beautiful, too). These cutting-edge designs are striking, joyful and fun. I demonstrate that everlasting flowers can be turned into modern, sustainable floral art that has the power to bring nature inside and uplift the spirits at any time of year.

In this book you will find 28 of my most successful everlasting floral designs. They are explained in three colour-themed chapters – brights, pastels and neutrals. In each chapter there is a mixture of simple to slightly more challenging options to make sure there's something for those of all skill levels. In each design, I'll talk you through the flowers, materials and tools you'll need, and then go on to explain the steps to create the structure of the design and how to decorate it to create a unique, head-turning masterpiece.

The opening pages cover everything you need to know to get started. I share ideas for finding inspiration and the wonders of bringing nature indoors. I discuss where to source flowers to create with, followed by foraging tips. There is a flower directory illustrating the core flowers I use so that you can easily identify flower types and make individual choices. I explain my flower drying methods, so you can try drying your own. I show you all the tools and materials you'll need and there are some step-by-step techniques, so you can see in detail how to create your pieces (useful to refer back to). I also include a few ideas on how everlasting flowers can be used to influence a space.

You certainly don't need to be a pro (although you will still love this book if you are) or grow a million flowers to make the projects in this book. It's aimed to inspire everyone, from beginner to expert, from high-rise block to flower farm, and creatives and designers looking to make something different. Nor do you need to follow these designs to the letter – they are a guide to springboard from and embellish with your own style. I still learn as I go and encourage you to enjoy evolving the designs to create something special to you.

As well as the above, I hope this book conveys a few other, important points. These designs rival fresh flowers for their vibrancy, but totally knock the socks off them when it comes to how long they can last, making them an environmentally friendly alternative that can be enjoyed for years rather than days. Spending time in nature – particularly discovering wildflowers, textures and materials – brings into focus how rich and abundant our world is, and can only increase our appreciation and wonder of it. Using your hands and imagination can reveal the artist you have inside. And creating naturally beautiful interior décor can transform your home and infuse it with meaning. These flowers have power, and I hope you find as much pleasure in the whole process as I do.

Finding Inspiration

There are so many wonderful ways to find design inspiration. Think about what inspires you out in the wider world; what shapes, colours or styles of art do you find yourself drawn to?

I am inspired by the bittersweet juxtaposition of the stark mountains standing tall behind the lush, flower-filled valleys near my home. I love movement in my designs; the contrast between the wild, architectural elements and the colourful flowers. I also love bold lines and colours, with an industrial edge. Maybe you might like a repeat pattern that is cool, clean, neat and regular? Or hot, vibrant colours jostling next to one another?

I'm a strong believer in going with your inner creative spirit and would urge all of you to do so. This book is a guide to inspire your own designs, providing a starting point for your own creativity. Go outside, look around, think about the details you like and then translate them into your flower art. Make notes or a scrapbook of colours, textures or anything beautiful that catches your eye, and see if you can inject that essence into what you create.

The space

The intended space can be a big inspiration and, for me, this is often the starting point for a design. Here are a few aspects to consider:

- Where will the design be positioned? What feeling would you like it to bring to the space? How big/small, wild/neat or colourful/subtle do you want the design to be?

- What background will it have? Wall colour or texture can have a startling effect on how colours and materials appear. A dark background often makes colours ping, but can disguise dark twigs and delicate textures, so the design may need a few lighter shades to lift it. Light backgrounds show all the twiggy textures off beautifully. Coloured walls often enhance colour tones and create bold drama, which can be fun. Patterns and wall texture can diminish floral details and can be tricky to work with.

- Will it be in a light or shady position? If it's dimly lit, you may want to consider lighter colours that will show up more. Depending on the light source, it can be lovely to work with shadows and silhouettes in mind by choosing different structures and textures for light to filter through or illuminate.

- What other colours are around it? Picking up existing colour accents is a great way to plan a colour palette. Furnishings, such as sofas, rugs, cushions, art or wall colour, are all great places to look for colour pointers to base a design on.

- It can be great fun to re-create a spring, summer, autumn (fall) or winter theme to match the seasons.

Colour

You may already know what colours you are naturally drawn to. Personally, I love them all, with the many different characters that colour combinations can bring. Whites, pastels, brights, darks or neutrals, there is so much to enjoy. Whether you like calm whites or bold colours, they all have their place and can produce stunning effects. An all-white design can look wonderful in a minimalist setting, while a bright one can make a striking impact in the same space. Seek out colours that make you feel good and go with them.

Structure & texture

Choose a style depending on the situation. A clean, minimal flower panel in a neat frame can add colour and detail without dominating a room. A large, sprawling twiggy structure can add drama in a contemporary way.

Wild or neat

There is no right or wrong when it comes to how wild or controlled a design should be as both can be uniquely beautiful. A great tumble of vines, twigs and grasses can be very majestic, but, equally, an orchestrated, repeat design can be incredibly beautiful and effective. A wreath can be big and bushy or petite and delicate. A flower panel bursting with a solid colour or one made more like a gentle wildflower meadow are equally pleasing.

Symmetry

A delicate balance between symmetry and random variation is required to make a piece flow and pull together, even when working to an asymmetric concept. I find that all my designs need a certain amount of careful symmetry to work, just like a well-composed photograph or picture. Saying that, too much symmetry can kill the character and make a design feel static and stiff, so somewhere in the middle is what I recommend.

Benefits of Using Everlasting Flowers

Over the years, I've realized there are many benefits to working with and creating dried floral art.

Nature makes us feel good

It can be truly mesmerizing how a piece of everlasting flower art can transform a room, drawing your eye and changing the atmosphere with its organic form. Just like gazing at a lovely meadow full of wildflowers, seeing this natural beauty can fill us with a sense of calm, happiness and wellbeing. Various scientific studies have shown that houseplants have mental health benefits, such as improving mood, reducing stress and improving attention span. I would argue that everlasting flowers are the same! Just like a bouquet of flowers or a leafy houseplant, everlasting flowers create a feeling of life, wonder and movement within a space.

Telling a story

Another unexpected but delightful aspect of gathering and making with dried materials, is the meaning it can give to the plants and flowers that have been collected along the way. This may be in the form of wedding flowers or plants kept from another special occasion. In my case, it can be a handful of flowers or driftwood foraged on a happy holiday or a place with good memories, or something given to me by a friend. All these little scraps of nature lovingly used together tell a wonderful story when woven into a piece of floral art, giving it extra special depth every time you look at it.

Sustainability

Drying and using your own flowers is sustainable in a number of multifaceted ways.

To my eye, everlasting floral art matches up to a bunch of bright, fresh flowers, and lasts considerably longer. A bunch of fresh flowers may only last a week, while a dried bouquet can last for years.

Foraging responsibly, growing your own flowers or sourcing flowers locally can eliminate the need for flower travel, and often means they will be organically grown, too. This makes it a far more sustainable way of enjoying flower decoration.

Out of season colour is delightful. Using everlasting flowers means being able to enjoy bright colours all year round, even in the depths of winter, without buying air-flown flowers from a warmer climate.

The materials I use are mostly natural and compostable, with the exception of wire, which can be re-cycled or reused. You can use natural twine or string in place of wire for fully compostable work.

It's easy to rejuvenate a dried floral piece with a few new dried flowers here and there to keep it looking bright and fresh. (Although personally, in most cases, I enjoy the gradual fading that the flowers undergo, gently revealing a softer character that can be lovely at different stages). You can also re-use a flower panel frame or wreath base to save making a new one.

Sourcing Flowers

Finding flowers to work with can be an exciting adventure. My brain has become finely attuned to spotting potential material for drying in just about any situation. Friends and family often laugh at my obsessive dedication to my art, knowing that they are highly likely to end up being roped into aiding me in some way. I hope I can infuse you with some of this passion.

Grow your own

This is by far the most rewarding and fun way to fully enjoy the whole dried-flower process. By growing your own, you get to choose what colours and textures you want, and have the potential to harvest the quantities you need. For me, it has many more benefits, such as getting outdoors and being fully in touch with what I am making. Knowing that my flowers are grown organically, to promote wildlife and don't need to travel are other huge bonuses. Whether you just grow a few flowers from seed in pots on a balcony, gather from an existing perennial garden or get into growing on a larger scale, I urge you to try it and experience the benefits.

Local flower growers

If you are not growing your own, I recommend acquiring flowers from local growers. Whether you buy from a market, local farm or small-scale grower, I have found the quality and varieties sourced this way second to none. I bought bucketfuls of glorious organic ranunculi from a local flower grower when my own crop failed. It felt great knowing I was supporting a local business, as well as ethical growing methods.

Shop bought

This can be a convenient way to obtain both dried flowers and fresh flowers that you can then dry at home when you are starting out. Supermarkets, garden centres and florists are all useful sources, and can be a fun way of experimenting. I would always urge consideration of where the flowers have come from and try to choose flowers that are as sustainable as possible.

Wholesale suppliers

These tend to be online and offer bulk discounts for professional florists. In most instances you will be required to create a business account to buy from them and may need to be a registered business. It can be a valuable way to source large quantities of flowers for big projects when lots of repeated colours or textures are needed.

Online

There are an increasing number of online dried-flower suppliers, which is good news because it means there are more and more everlasting flower varieties to choose from. I find these very useful when I need a few more specific flowers for a job and I don't have enough of my own. Online marketplaces such as Etsy or eBay can be a good place to look, too, often providing unusual or interesting dried flowers from small-scale growers that may even be local to you.

Foraging

This is an amazing way to boost your flower palette, save money and fully appreciate how awesome nature is. For more, see pages 18–19.

Friends

Friends can be a brilliant way of sourcing flowers for drying or seeds for growing. I have been given some beautiful and unusual gems from other people. Whether it's flowers from their gardens, something they've foraged or even flowers they've purchased that have dried beautifully, friends can add some valuable finds to your collection.

Foraging

Areas of wasteland, roadside verges and wild areas of our gardens often contain a wealth of potential material for everlasting flower design. Once you get your eye in and truly appreciate the individual colours and textures to be found in nature, you'll be hooked. These wild elements are an integral part of my designs, often providing the structure, background and finer details that enhance the bolder colours.

What to look out for

Foraging in the wild brings an appreciation of each season. It's a joy to gather different materials as the months pass; collecting, drying and storing treasure to use in the year ahead. Winter is the time for finding twigs and branches, while they are leafless and their outline is clear to see. Spring and summer bring an abundance of flowers. In autumn (fall) you can collect leaves, grasses, berries, nuts and seeds. There is nearly always something to be found, so have fun discovering what grows around you.

BOUGHS

I always keep my eyes peeled for interesting twigs and branches. Finding a beautiful piece of wood can be the starting point for a design. Old, contorted ivy boughs are great, as are many other tree branches. It's worth keeping a collection if you have the space. Gather willow, birch, hazel and other woody material in winter while they are leafless, and store under cover for future use.

LEAVES

Leaves, such as fern and bracken, as well as oak, beech and many others, are a wonderful element to add to the everlasting flower palette. Gather them at different stages of development to achieve a variety of colours. Press between sheets of cardboard to dry and save for later.

GRASSES

Wild grasses offer an incredibly beautiful array of textures, colours and shapes. They add a delicate, wild elegance to any design. Picking grasses at different stages of maturity throughout the season is a great way to achieve an even wider range of colours and textures.

SEED HEADS

The silhouettes, outlines and textures of seedheads are architectural and statuesque, so form a key compenent in many designs. Flowers such as hogweed, jack-by-the-hedge, dock, shepherd's purse, wild carrot, nipplewort and pine cones are just a small example of what can be found.

VINES

Honeysuckle and other creepers can provide brilliant foundation material for wreaths and other structures. The glorious, fluffy seed heads of traveller's joy are second to none for their light-catching, whimsical charm in the winter months.

FLOWERS AND BERRIES

Depending on where you are in the world, this selection will vary wildly. Here in the UK, I pick armfuls of meadow buttercups (which dry amazingly), bistort, yarrow, sneezewort, sea statice and more. In autumn (fall) I collect rowan berries, which dry and keep well, plus hips and spindle for a more limited but beautiful show.

Foraging guidelines

While we may love the idea of free wildflowers, we must remember that they are part of an ecosystem, providing food and a habitat for wildlife, as well as setting seed for future plants. My rule of thumb is to pick considerately and carefully, taking a little from a wide area. The art of foraging well is that no one can tell you were ever there. Wildflowers are for everyone to enjoy, so always get permission to forage on other

people's property, and never pick from nature reserves, protected areas of natural beauty, public spaces or other people's gardens. Most of what I forage is either from the areas I've let run wild in my own garden or roadside verges that will be cut anyway.

REMEMBER

- Only take a small amount of what's there.
- Tread carefully and pick gently so that you leave the area as you found it.
- Never forage from nature reserves or protected areas.
- Don't pick from gardens or private property without prior permission.
- Leave flowers that may upset others if they were taken, such as verges next to other people's property.
- Take care near busy roads; park and pick safely and responsibly.
- Follow the regional foraging laws and guidelines relevant to you.

TIPS

- If you have a garden, leave a small section of lawn uncut to create your own wild foraging area.
- Once you have gathered your branches and vines, keep them dry and undercover - then they can last for years.
- Use nature as inspiration for design ideas. Look for shapes, colours and textures that ignite your imagination. Take a few notes and pictures to help capture the moment.

Directory of Flowers & Boughs

In this directory, I have included a selection of the flowers I love and use most often in my work after many years of trial and error. I have split the directory into different categories to help you identify where they may be used, but they are interchangeable and many look fabulous at all stages of decoration. I encourage you to try out your own combinations and substitute similar flowers and branches with ones you have to hand.

Grasses

Grasses have many uses in everlasting flower design. They are fantastic in the base layer of many projects, providing a natural, unobtrusive background that enhances the other flowers beautifully. They are also invaluable as a sparkle element, adding delicate movement and shimmer, which can bring a design alive.

Feather reed grass, *Calamagrostis* x *acutiflora* 'Karl Foerster'

Common reed grass, *Phragmites australis*

Foxtail millet grass (red), *Setaria italica* 'Red Jewel'; wild foxtail millet grass (green), *Setaria viridis*

Greater quaking grass, *Briza maxima*

Bunny tail grass, *Lagurus ovatus*

Wild grasses such as: Yorkshire fog, *Holcus lanatus*; soft brome, *Bromus hordeaceus*; reed sweet-grass, *Glyceria maxima*; cocksfoot grass, *Dactylis glomerata*; meadow foxtail, *Alopecurus pratensis*; false oat-grass, *Arrhenatherum elatius*

Squirrel tail grass, *Hordeum jubatum*

Cloud grass, *Agrostis nebulosa*

Filler flowers

Filler flowers are the bedrock of any design. They provide the framework and substance that the showier flowers hang upon. They also provide a wealth of stunning textures, colours and shapes that can be used in many combinations to create a whole range of styles.

Bracken, *Pteridium aquilinum*; fern, *Dryopteris affinis*

Field pennycress, *Thlaspi arvense* 'Green Bell'

Feverfew, *Tanacetum parthenium* 'Tetra White'

Honesty, *Lunaria annua*

German statice, *Goniolimon tataricum*

Annual statice, *Limonium sinuatum*

Red amaranth (upright), *Amaranthus cruentus*; love-lies-bleeding (trailing), *Amaranthus caudatus*

Hydrangea, *Hydrangea macrophylla*

Winged everlasting, *Ammobium alatum*

Astrantia, *Astrantia major*

Golden clusters, *Rhodanthe humboldtiana*

Persian cress, *Lepidium sativum*

Lady's mantle, *Alchemilla mollis*

Larkspur, *Delphinium consolida*

Velvetleaf, *Abutilon theophrasti*

Eucalyptus (small, green leafed), *Eucalyptus parvifolia*; eucalyptus (large, silver leafed), *Eucalyptus cinerea*

Sea holly, *Eryngium planum*

Pearly everlasting, *Anaphalis margaritacea*

Pennycress, *Thlaspi arvense*

Yellow ageratum, *Lonas inodora*

Star flowers

The star flowers are the showstoppers, the jewels in the crown. Often applied later in a design so that they can be clearly seen, these blooms bring definition, depth and fabulous punches of colour and texture.

Globe thistle, *Echinops bannaticus*

Chinese lanterns, *Alkekengi officinarum*

Strawflower, *Xerochrysum bracteatum*

African marigold, *Tagetes erecta*

Peony, *Paeonia spp.*

Paper daisy, *Helipterum roseum*

Roses, *Rosa spp.* (fully double varieties such as 'James Galway', 'Port Sunlight' and 'The Queen of Sweden')

Cornflower, *Centaurea cyanus*

Dahlia, *Dahlia spp.* (pompom and mid-sized double varieties)

Poppy head, *Papaver somniferum*

Ranunculus, *Ranunculus asiaticus*

Sparkle flowers

These little flowers have magical qualities. Applied at the very end, these delicate beauties lift a design and make it sparkle. A few well-placed, tiny pops of colour here and there enhance the other flowers, while escaping whisps and fronds provide subtle depth and bring a design to completion.

Bistort, *Bistorta officinalis* 'Superba' or *Bistorta amplexicaulis*

Billy button, *Craspedia globosa*

Pink poker statice, *Limonium suworowii*

Buttercup, *Ranunculus acris*

Immortelle, *Xeranthemum annuum*

Shepherd's purse, *Capsella bursa-pastoris*

Wood & vine

Wood and vines create the structure, background and frame of most designs. This is where many projects start. It is also very important for providing the wild and slightly tougher elements that give a piece an edge. These textures bring lots of movement that makes a design feel striking and full of character.

Hazel, *Corylus avellana*

Willow, *Salix cinerea*

Birch, *Betula pendula*

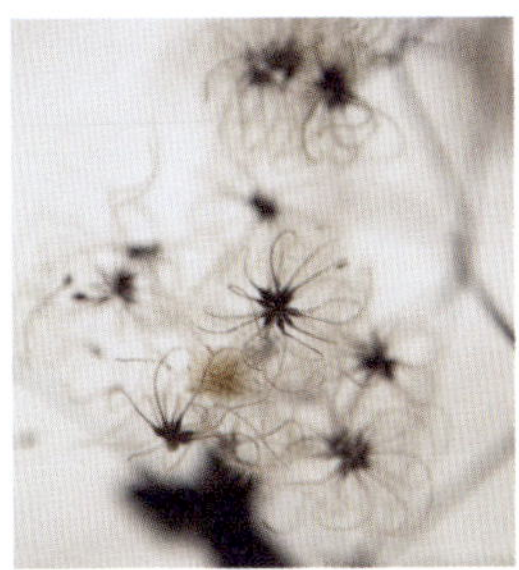

Traveller's joy, *Clematis vitalba*

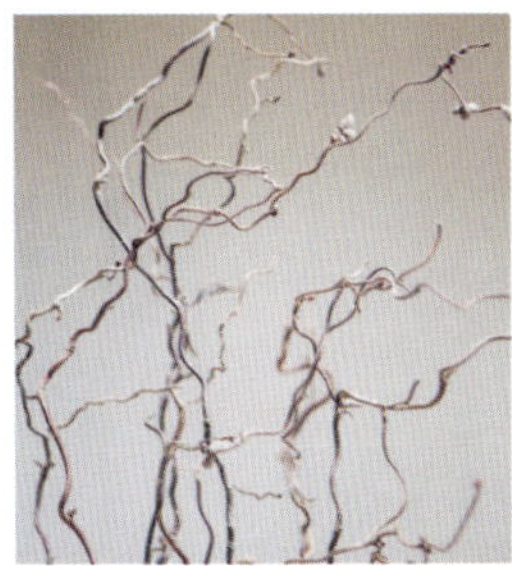

Corkscrew hazel, *Corylus avellana* 'Contorta'

Drying Flowers

Drying your own flowers opens a whole new world of discovery and potential as to what you can create. I have such fun drying different plants and am always on the lookout for something new to test or experimenting with harvesting at different stages. It really is very addictive. Whether you are growing your own flowers or buying them in fresh, foraging or even drying an old bouquet you don't want to waste, using this natural, air-drying method is incredibly simple, effective and fun to do.

What to dry

There are lots of well-known flower varieties that lend themselves well to drying; buttercups and cornflowers, for example, which hold their shape and colour beautifully. However, not all flowers dry successfully. Phlox and lilies, for example, simply shrivel up and go brown. It can be fun to see what works. Here are a few categories of flowers and boughs that I have had success with:

- Common annuals sown every year, such as strawflowers, paper daisies, pennycress, cornflowers, larkspur and many others.
- Biennials, like honesty, that flower the year after sowing and self-seed wonderfully.
- Perennials that flower year after year, such as globe thistle, sea holly, lady's mantle, billy button, grasses and astrantia.
- Bulbs and corms providing magnificent dahlia, ranunculus, allium, narcissi and other beauties.
- Shrubs providing flowers and foliage, such as hydrangea, pittosporum or box.
- Climbing plants, such as traveller's joy, hop bines, vines and Virginia creeper, which are all brilliant, wiggly characters, great for wreath bases and adding extra detail.
- Trees, such as willow, birch, hazel, eucalyptus, rowan and more, form an important category of dried flower work that many may not think about.

If you intend to create detailed work from your flowers, it's worth thinking about the different roles the flowers play. Having some background and filler flowers, as well as the bright showy ones is worth considering before you start your drying journey in order to end up with a mixed palette. See 'Sourcing flowers' (pages 14-15), for more on where to get your flowers from.

When to pick

Unlike fresh flowers, which are best picked in the coolest part of the day, everlasting flowers need to be picked when they are bone dry for the best results. If not, moisture can get trapped inside the petals and the flowers will go mouldy in the drying process; I have learned the hard way with this. Pick after the morning dew has lifted and the flowers are totally free of damp.

Different flowers benefit from being picked at different stages of development so that they dry well. Generally, most flowers can be picked as soon as they have opened and are in perfect condition, before they have been bleached by the sun. This way the colours remain brighter after drying. There are a few exceptions to this, such as pink poker statice, red amaranth, pennycress, hydrangea, astrantia and honesty, which need to harden off and become 'papery' before they will dry well.

TIPS

- Hang bunches of flowers from coat hangers placed in a cupboard or wardrobe as a simple storage solution.
- Grow a few everlasting flowers in pots if you don't have a garden. Immortelle, paper daisies and bunny tail grass work well.
- Pennycress, peonies, cornflowers, statice, sea holly and billy buttons are a few great flowers to buy fresh and then dry at home.
- Pick bracken, leaves and grasses at different times of year so you have both green and brown options to dry.

Drying methods

I dry all my flowers with a simple air-dry method. It's very easy and is an entirely natural process that requires no chemicals. An ideal drying place is a warm, dry ceiling or a wall away from direct light. A garden shed or outbuilding is not usually suitable unless you live in a hot, dry country. Any damp will quickly ruin dried flowers, so having a consistently dry atmosphere is essential. I use my studio ceiling, which is wooden and has many hooks to hang flowers from. If you don't have a ceiling space to use, you could create a frame to hang flowers from. Hanging flowers along a nice characterful branch can also look great, saving the need for so many hooks in walls and ceilings.

AIR-DRY METHOD

1 Strip any unwanted leaves from the stems before you dry them to make it easier to tie them into bunches and reduce the chance of mould forming in the drying process.

2 Tie the flowers into smallish bunches so that the flower heads are not squashing each other and they dry quickly. I use natural jute garden twine, which is re-usable and compostable. Wrap it around the stems a couple of times towards the cut stem ends and tie firmly. Tie the twine ends together to create a hanging loop.

3 Hang the flower bunches upside down, so the stem ends are at the top and the flower heads are at the bottom. This will allow the flowers to dry with nice straight stems.

4 Leave a little space between the bunches to allow good air circulation around them.

5 Drying time varies depending on the conditions and the types of flowers, but it usually takes two to five weeks. Once dried, the flowers should feel papery to the touch and the stems should be firm when held upright.

OTHER DRYING METHODS

There are a few other drying techniques that can sometimes be useful.

- Place the flowers in a vase with a small amount of water in the bottom, so that the flowers dry upright and very gradually. This allows the flowers to open and firm up as they dry, and can be useful for flowers such as hydrangea.

- Thread stems, flower heads up, through a chicken wire grill that supports the flower head in an open position as it dries. This can be good for large flower heads where you don't want the petals to fold in on themselves, as would happen if they were upside down.

- Press bracken, fern and flat leaves between sheets of cardboard until dry.

Storing flowers

How you store flowers once they are dry is key to having colourful, well-formed blooms. As with drying, a completely moisture-free atmosphere is essential. Somewhere dark or very low light is also preferable to prevent colour fading. Here are some options:

- Hanging bunches upside down. Once the flowers are completely dry, they can be hung closer together to save space. I store most of my flowers this way, from hooks under deep shelving, which allows good visibility and access.

- Upright in buckets and containers. This is great for plants with firm stems that won't gradually wilt, such as pennycress, lady's mantle, field pennycress and grasses, but not so good for strawflowers or others that can flop gradually when stored in this way.

- In boxes and lidded tubs. This is the method I use the least because, over time, the weight of the flowers slowly flattens them and can ruin their shape. However, it is an excellent way to store grasses, fern and bracken, and can work well for individual flower heads (such as strawflowers), a few delicate, lighter flower types (such as pink poker statice) or more robust varieties (such as globe thistles).

How Everlasting Flowers Influence a Space

I still get such a kick out of how much everlasting flowers can transform a space. They have so much character and can be used in so many ways to bring dramatic effect, as well as much pleasure and joy. There aren't many places that a piece of everlasting floral art won't sit beautifully in a home. I have made garlands for bathrooms, flower hearts for bedrooms, wreaths for kitchens, flower panels for sitting rooms, flower clouds for stairwells and bouquets for sideboards. The possibilities are endless. Damp can be a consideration in some situations; if you are concerned about it, choose twigs and robust flowers and textures that can stand up better to moisture.

Table styling

There are so many exciting ways to dress a table for a unique dining experience. From simple delicate stems in small vases to full-on banquet displays, adding flowers to a table always looks beautiful. You could also try hanging a flower cloud or sculpture above a table, or garlands, flower vines or wreaths on the walls around a table to create a striking atmosphere.

Window dressing

Flower panels, flower clouds, blossom branches, bouquets and flower displays are all wonderful ways to make windows look fabulous. They will need to look good from both inside and outside. It is worth remembering that flowers placed in a window will fade much faster than normal flowers due to the light and heat levels, but I think it is still well worth it for a beautiful display for all to see and enjoy. You can expect to get a year out of them before they fade too much.

Room dividers

Flower panels, everlasting blossom trees or hanging flower sculptures are a great way of gently dividing a space while still allowing light through interiors.

Ceiling décor

Hanging sculptures are a fantastic way to enhance ceiling areas – particularly tall, empty spaces – and create amazing impact and drama. They look great in tents and marquees, above stages, in dining halls, stairwells and windows – just about anywhere that you can stand back and appreciate the spectacle of a beautiful hanging flower sculpture. I have had the same circular twig and flower sculpture above my kitchen table for over five years now, and still get many compliments on it.

Wall art

Wall art is a special passion of mine. I love the way it brings wild, architectural character to a room. It's possible to achieve a lot of impact from a simple palette of colours and materials. The organic nature of these wall sculptures makes them brilliant for adapting to many different situations, providing striking, unique décor and dramatic points of focus. They are perfect for decorating above fireplaces or bed heads, in hallways and stairwells or curved around doorways and windows.

Tools & Equipment

I have a selection of much-used tools, but it's not vast or fancy. When I first started out, I only had a pair of secateurs, some blunt pliers for wire cutting and a wood saw, which were all perfectly adequate until I managed to collect a better set over time. I've mentioned some alternatives where possible. The same applies to materials; there are no hard and fast rules. Simply adapt what you have available.

Tools

FLORISTRY SCISSORS ❶

Floristry scissors are my trusty friends. I have several pairs, so that I always have some close at hand, even in the car, in my bag and in my coat pocket. There is nothing worse than seeing something I desperately want to pick in a hedgerow and not being able to! Over the years I have tried a few different scissor brands, but the scissors I like the most are made by US-based company Barnel. They have light, sharp, fine-tipped, stainless-steel blades, with a serrated section at the base that are superb for cutting fine wire and woody stems, which set them apart and make them ideal for this job.

SECATEURS ❷

I also have a pair of secateurs for cutting thicker, woodier stems, which are great for cutting willow for frame making. If you only have a pair of secateurs to start with, they will adequately do the job of floristry scissors, too.

STURDY HOUSEHOLD SCISSORS ❸

Its handy to have a nice, sturdy, sharp pair of scissors for cutting cardboard (when making templates) or ribbons.

TAPE MEASURE ❹

This is an essential bit of kit. You will need it to measure the area where a floral artwork is to go, to help decide what size design to make. Use it when creating the mechanics of your design, such as the template, wreath base or willow rods for a frame, as well as measuring how large a wreath or flower display is becoming as you make it.

PRUNING LOPPERS ❺

These are a long, double-handled, robust version of secateurs for cutting thick branches. I use mine to cut hazel (when making everlasting blossom trees) and ivy branches (for wall art). A wood saw would be a suitable alternative.

WIRE CUTTERS ❻

Required for cutting chicken wire and thicker wires, like rustic vine wire. A good, sharp pair of wire cutters make cutting a pleasure, while a blunt, rusty, stiff pair make it tedious. If you have an adequate pair of pliers with a wire cutting section, these can work fine, too – they are just a little fiddlier to use.

PEN/PENCIL ❼

Needed for marking out cardboard templates.

AWL ❽

I use this as a centre pin to hold twine when scribing a circular outline on card for round template making. Any pointed large pin will do, even a sharp pencil.

LARGE NEEDLE ❾

Used for threading twine through strawflowers. You will need a needle head large enough to thread garden twine through its eye. A wool darning needle is ideal.

Materials

CHICKEN WIRE ❿

I use this versatile metal fabric as the basis of many of my flower designs. I love its silver honeycomb texture and its slightly industrial, modern feel. Originally invented as animal fencing, it is a strong, galvanized-steel, hexagonal mesh, that is pliable and can be moulded into different shapes. After trying out many different sizes, I now tend to use one gauge size, which has 13mm (½in) hexagons, as I find it works best for most things. However, you can use other sizes.

BINDING WIRE ⓫

I call this magic wire. It is useful for so many things when working with everlasting flowers. It is thin, strong, easy to use and blends into the background beautifully so that it is hardly noticeable afterwards. I use the black annealed version, but it also comes in green and silver.

BULLION WIRE ⓬

This is a thinner, more delicate wire, that comes in many colours. Its brilliant for making flower strands, supporting delicate stems and general flower fixing. It has a crinkled texture, which makes it incredibly effective at gripping stems, as well as creating a glittery effect as it moves in the light. I use the silver version for most of my work, but love the other colours, too.

RUSTIC VINE WIRE ⓭

A thick wire, covered in a textured jute coating. It comes in dark brown, green and beige colours, and is brilliant for flower crowns, or where a strong, sinewy background is needed.

CARDBOARD ⓮

I use the sides of old cardboard boxes to make templates. The card needs to be strong enough to cope with chicken wire being bent up around it in the frame-making process.

TWINE ⓯

A natural-coloured, compostable garden string ideal for tying around bunches of flowers when drying, securing bundles of willow rods, circular template making and flower strings. It can also be used as a compostable substitute for wire in project construction. It comes in many other colours, perfect for simple bouquet or buttonhole binding.

ROPE ⓰

A natural 6mm (¼in) thick compostable rustic rope or sash cord is useful for doubling up to create garland bases or for general construction.

RIBBON

A length of special ribbon can elevate everlasting flowers to another level. Whether for a bouquet, flower crown or wreath, it's a lovely addition. I have a drawer full of different sizes, colours and textures so I can try out different options to find what looks best.

CIRCULAR HOOPS ⓱

Use these pre-made metal or wooden hoops for making the central backing for wall sculptures or as circular flower panel frames to save time.

POT TAPE ⓲

Pot tape is a super sticky, waterproof tape used for sticking things down to the sides of pots and vases. There are clear and green versions. Clear tape is great when it is more likely to be seen, but is not as sticky as the green tap. So, I'd recommend the green tape for bigger jobs, where extra adhesion is required.

Flower vessels

VASES

These can be jugs, pots, urns or whatever you like. Choose something that complements the flowers and is a good size for the ultimate flower arrangement.

BOWLS

Bowls are a brilliant way of displaying everlasting flowers when keeping the display low is key. Any bowls can be used, even cereal bowls if you like them.

FOOTED BOWLS

Rather like a bowl with a little pedestal, footed bowls elevate a flower display slightly, bringing a sense of elegance, and are great where height isn't an issue.

MINI VASES AND BOTTLES

I have a lovely collection of small vases and bottles that I've acquired over the years. They are so useful for displaying dried flowers where individual stems can be appreciated and a light, airy look is required.

PIN FROG ⓳

Small, weighty, round metal discs, with a bed of sharp steel, brass or copper pins sticking up from the base. They can be placed in a bowl or vase or used on their own to provide a minimal, elegant way of holding collections of individual flower stems in position, either by wedging the stems between the pins or inserting the pins inside the base of hollow stems.

10
5
11
17
15
12
13
2
7
15
1
6
3
4
BAHCO
9
18
19
8
16
14

Techniques

This following pages bring together a few essential but simple techniques that I have developed to construct my flower designs.

Attach & secure wire to projects

ATTACH A PIECE OF WIRE TO GET STARTED

You can either wrap the wire around whatever you are about to work on and firmly twist several times. A

Or you can wrap the wire around what you are working on and tie a firm knot, as you might with a piece of string. B

JOIN A NEW PIECE OF WIRE

1 Take the new length of wire and cross it over the end of the existing piece.

2 Twist the wire ends together in opposite directions.

3 Make sure you twist enough times to make it secure so it won't pull apart easily; roughly ten twists should do it nicely.

SECURE THE END OF THE WIRE

Leave enough wire to tie off your end – approximately 20cm (8in) is good. Make a small loop to one side of the attaching point and, with the end of the wire, double back under and pull out on the other side. C

You will now have two strands that you can twist together to secure. D

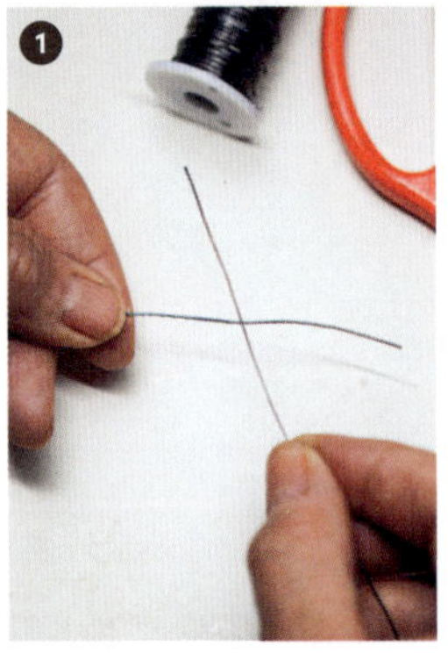

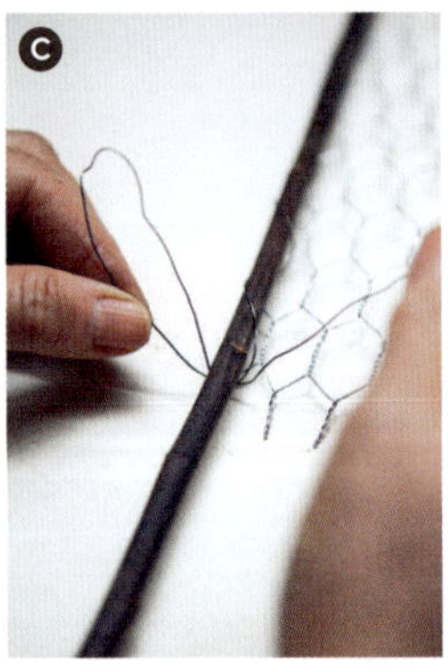

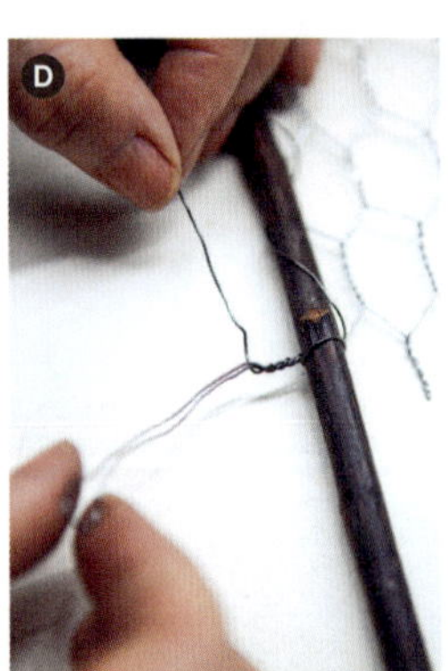

Attach wire to flowers

WIRE A FLOWER HEAD

1 Cut a length of binding wire – approximately 20cm (8in) should do. Cut the ends of the wire at an angle to create a sharp point. Push one end of the wire through the front of the flower head, slightly to one side where it is softer, taking care not to stab the supporting fingers behind. Pull the wire one third of the way through.

2 Take the remaining end of wire, bend it over and push through the flower head 0.5cm (¼in) away from the previous wire. Pull the wire through the back of the flower head all the way down, gently but firmly embedding the wire into the flower head.

3 Now twist the two ends together behind the flower head to secure the wire.

ATTACH TO BRANCH

Wire a flower head (steps 1–3 above). Continue winding the wires together to form a stalk. It is now ready to be wired into your project. D

ATTACH TO WREATH

Wire a flower head (steps 1–3 above), using a slightly longer piece of binding wire. Loop the wire halfway back up on itself and twist together. This creates a firm wire stem to push into a wreath. E

ATTACH TO MESH

1 Place a length of bullion wire over the front of the flower head – approximately 20cm (8in). Gently tease the wire down the sides between the petals so that the wire is hidden nicely. Gently push the wire into the centre of the flower with a thumbnail to help to blend it in. Pull the wire gently but firmly to the centre at the back of the flower, and either tie or twist together. F

2 The wire ends can then be used to wire directly onto the mesh. Pull the wire ends around whatever you are attaching to and twist them firmly together to secure. G

1

2

3

D

E

F

G

STRENGTHEN A STEM

For delicate stems, wire a flower head as you did in step 1 of 'attach to mesh' (see page 39). Then wrap the wire ends gently down the length of the stem to provide additional support. H

WIRE FLOWER STRANDS

1 Prepare the flowers you are to use by cutting the stems to approximately 1.5cm (½in) long. You will need one flower for every 5–10cm (2–4in) of wire used.

2 Cut a length of bullion wire to the length you need, plus a little extra for attaching afterwards. Before you start wiring, decide the order of the flowers. Start with the one you want to appear at the top of the strand and wrap the wire gently but firmly around the stem three or four times. Repeat this process with the rest of the flower heads, adding them every 5–10cm (2–4in) along the length of the wire. I

Attach flowers to chicken wire

WEAVE FLOWERS IN

The main principle behind attaching flowers to chicken wire is to simply weave the flower stems in and out of the honeycomb wire holes enough times to hold firm. This is a versatile, easy method that allows you to make changes whenever you want and build up the layers of a beautiful design.

1 Start by holding the flower head/stem up against the front of the panel, moving it around until you are happy with its position.

2 Using your finger, mark the hole where the flower head sits.

3 With the flower in the other hand, weave the stem down from that point, gently pulling it into position so the head sits snuggly into the initial hole you started with. I recommend threading the stems in and out three to five times, or even more for fine-stemmed grasses. This way, they should hold well.

4 Dried flower stems can be brittle, some more than others, so be gentle but firm while weaving. The further apart the holes you weave in and out of, the less it will put pressure on the stem, therefore reducing the risk of it snapping. It's a delicate balance of finding just the right amount of tension to curve the stems in and out without breaking. This takes a bit of getting used to, so don't worry if you snap one or two, you will get a feel for it with practice.

5 Once you are happy with the flower's position, trim off any stem that protrudes beyond the frame base.

ADD EXTRA SUPPORT

Occasionally, flowers will need a bit of extra support to strengthen the stem and prevent the head from snapping off, especially if they have thin or droopy necks. In these cases, extra support using bullion wire is a good idea. See 'strengthen a stem' (page 40), then thread the stem as usual.

ATTACH STEMLESS FLOWER HEADS

Using flower heads with no stem can be very effective, and a great way to use up short-stemmed or stemless flowers. The result can be slightly less natural than the stemmed weaving, giving a flatter look, it still looks great. See 'attach to mesh' (page 39), then thread the wires through to the back of the frame and either tie or twist the wire to secure.

ATTACH SHORT-STEMMED FLOWERS AND BRACKEN FRONDS

For bracken fronds, short-stemmed flowers or to attach flowers at the base of a panel where there is no weaving space, direct wiring onto the frame is recommended. To do this, cut a short length of bullion wire, approximately 8cm (3in) will do. Position it over the front of your flower stem and push both ends through the chicken wire to the back and then tie or twist together to secure. Use one or two pieces of wire per stem as needed. J

1

2

3

4

8

5

Make a willow wreath base

A wreath base is basically just a long, thin willow sausage wired together and bent into a circle. The longer and thicker the sausage, the bigger the circle, so these instructions can be applied to any size wreath with a bit of adjustment. You will need a bundle of dry brown willow rods in varying thicknesses, depending on your wreath size. Generally, a length of 1m (40in) and a thickness of 3–7mm (⅛–¼ in) is good in most cases, but very large wreaths will need to be thicker to compensate.

1 To start, select two or three willow rods, placing the cut ends together. Use a combination of rod thicknesses both now and throughout the making process to allow an even circle bend. Fix the end of a reel of binding wire near the tips, keeping it attached to the spool.

2 Holding the willow and the reel of wire in your non-dominant hand, pick up two or three more willow rods with your dominant hand, and place them at staggered intervals along the existing willow, tucking the ends in, and working away from the cut ends. Bind the wire around the willow twice, 2–3cm (1–2in) apart to hold it together, and repeat. Keep a medium wire tension as you go. You will need to be able to push your flower stems in under the wire when decorating, and it can be a nightmare if it's too tight!

3 Repeat this process with two or three new rods at a time, moving along to create a willow sausage approximately 3–4cm (1–1½in) thick. When you have wired roughly a 1m (40in) length, stop and try for size, leaving the remaining willow ends unbound for now.

4 Take the butt end firmly in your non-dominant hand and the feathery end in the other, then bend the butt end around in a circle and wedge it into the inside side of your sausage. There can be quite a bit of tension in the bound willow at this stage, so be prepared to use a bit of muscle! The butt end should curve round to roughly match up with where you have wired to.

5 Bend the feathery ends around the outside of your hoop, making up an even thickness by overlapping the two tapering ends to form an even circle. Hold together while you check for size with a tape measure, sliding the ends in or out to adjust the size if needed. Release and add more willow if it's not quite big enough.

6 Once you are happy with the size, hold the willow circle ends firmly together with your non-dominant hand, and continue wrapping wire around until all the ends are bound and secure (remembering not to bind it too tightly).

7 Check the hoop shape. Use your knee or foot to gently push out from the inside to help round it off where necessary.

8 Now you have a beautiful willow circle, it's time to add an extra layer of binding wire for the flower fixing. Attach a reel of wire, winding it around the willow ring repeatedly every 1cm (½in) all the way round, remembering not to make it too tight so the flower stems can easily slide under it.

9 Finally attach a 15cm (6in) loop of wire at the top of the willow ring to hang it from.

1

BRIGHTS

Bright & Wild Wreath

If I were to say I had an iconic wreath to my name, this would be it. Invented over years of experimenting with different colour and texture combinations, this has evolved to be my most popular design. It defies the conventional concept of muted, rustic-coloured dried-flower arrangements and traditional Christmas wreaths, instead being a bright, fun, creative flower circle perfect for many a space with its long-lasting beauty at any time of year.

Perfect for

- Above fireplaces
- Sitting rooms or lounges
- Hallways
- Kitchens
- Bedrooms
- Walls
- Around mirrors
- Table centrepieces
- Doors
- Window displays

Tools & equipment

- Floristry scissors/secateurs
- Tape measure
- Binding wire

Flowers & boughs

Boughs

- 1 x bundle willow rods, 0.5cm (¼in) thick, or similar flexible stems for the base ring
- 5 x birch branch

Filler flowers

- 8 x field pennycress
- 5 x feverfew
- 5 x German statice
- 3 x annual statice, yellow
- 3 x annual statice, pink
- 1–2 x honesty
- 15 x fern
- 5 x Persian cress
- 3 x sea holly
- 20 x larkspur, blue and pink

Show flowers

- 60 x strawflower, mixture of colours
- 8 x globe thistle
- 30 x paper daisy, pink
- 10 x paper daisy, white

Sparkle flowers

- 10 x billy button
- 20 x immortelle, purple
- 15 x cornflower, blue
- 20 x winged everlasting
- 15 x wild grass
- 15 x bunny tail grass
- 10 x shepherd's purse
- 10 x pink poker statice

Method

MAKE THE BACKGROUND STRUCTURE

1 Make a base ring from the willow rods, following the instructions on pages 42–43.

2 Cut a handful of birch (or similar) twig tips of varying lengths, from 10–50cm (4–20in) depending on how they come off the branch, with the secateurs. Cut at an angle to create a pointed tip.

3 Push the cut birch ends under the willow ring wires, wedging them in between the willow rods until you can feel them grip securely in place. It may take a couple of attempts to find a sweet spot that works. I tend to place the twigs in one direction as I work, creating a loose wheel effect that has a flow to it.

4 Continue cutting a handful of twigs at a time and adding them to your wreath, around both the outside and inside edges of the ring, until you have an even, well-structured twiggy covering. Stand back to check the overall balance from a distance and from each side to make sure it looks good from every angle. Make sure there are enough twigs at the back, too.

DECORATE THE FILLER LAYER

5 The filler background layer is where the main body of the wreath is created. Start with the field pennycress. Cut varied lengths of 10–30cm (4–12in). Push the stem ends under the ring wires in between the birch, following the same angle and direction as the birch. Add them at irregular intervals of 10–20cm (4–8in) around the outside, then add a few smaller bits to the front and inner edge. Make sure they are lodged firmly in place.

6 Repeat this process with the feverfew, German statice, annual statice and honesty along with the larkspur and Persian cress, varying the lengths and spacings to help give a sense of movement and depth to the design.

7 Cut the sea holly stems a little longer, to lengths of 30–40cm (12–18in), and position them strategically to stand out and add some drama.

8 Place the ferns evenly spaced at the back of the design.

9 Stand back, check the shape from a distance and make any necessary adjustments.

DECORATE THE SHOW LAYER

10 First, prepare the strawflowers. I pre-wire all my strawflowers for wreath making as it allows me to bend the heads in any direction, helping to achieve a natural look (see page 39). You can use them with their stems if you want to, it is just a bit trickier.

11 Push the strawflowers into place, working your way around the wreath. Hold the different colours up against your wreath as you work to see which colour combinations go well together. Insert a few flowers with slightly longer wire stems around the sides, too.

12 Once you have built up a nice, even layer of strawflowers, you can add the globe thistles and the paper daisies. Place a few around the sides and fill in all the gaps so that the wreath looks great from all angles.

13 Once again, stand back and view your wreath from a distance to check the overall shape for balance and colour, adding extra stems where needed.

DECORATE THE SPARKLE LAYER

14 Now that the main decoration is complete, it's time to inject a wild yet whimsical feel to it. For the finishing touches, add some acid-yellow billy buttons and immortelle, a sprinkling of blue cornflowers and some winged everlasting for a bit of contrast, followed by a few wild grasses, bunny tail grass and strands of shepherd's purse scattered throughout for added delicacy and beautiful silhouettes. At this stage, it can get very fiddly to try and push the stems in between the other flowers. Don't worry, take your time and enjoy working slowly, gently and methodically – this is just part of the process.

15 Finally, at the back, position a few evenly spaced pink poker statice, to create a firework effect.

16 Stand back one final time and see if any further stems are needed. At this stage, I often add a few more paper daisies if I can see any gaps that need colour, or a birch twig or two to bring balance to the outline.

TIPS

- To enhance the wild look or create more twig definition, add a few extra twigs at the back of your design.
- If your wreath is going to be placed in a slightly dark position, use a few more light colours to ensure it stands out.
- Placing the wreath on different walls as you work can help provide new perspectives of what it needs to make it look great.

Celebration Bouquet & Buttonhole

Whatever the celebration or event, flowers like these are the cherry on top of a special day, enhancing the beauty of whoever holds them. Putting time into making something extra special and long lasting like this bouquet and buttonhole is a great investment that can be enjoyed afterwards as a reminder of wonderful times. Topping all of that, they can be made in advance, sent in the post and will not wilt for those end-of-the-day photos.

Perfect for

- Weddings
- Ceremonies
- Tables
- Gifts
- Birthdays
- Home décor
- Parties and events
- Proms

Flowers & boughs

For the bouquet

- 5 x field pennycress
- 5 x German statice
- 7 x bracken frond
- 10–15 x winged everlasting
- 5 x sea lavender, purple
- 20 x cornflower, blue
- 20 x strawflower, golden
- 10 x paper daisy, pink
- 3 x billy button
- 10 x immortelle, purple
- 5 x dahlia, yellow
- 10 x strawflower, pink and orange
- 2 x globe thistle
- 3 x pink poker statice
- 10 x mixed wild grasses
- 3 x shepherd's purse

For the buttonhole

- 1 x fern frond
- 2 x wild grass
- 3 x German statice
- 1 x winged everlasting
- 1 x billy button
- 1 x globe thistle
- 1 x immortelle, purple
- 2 x strawflower, golden
- 1 x paper daisy, pink

Tools & equipment

- Floristry scissors/ secateurs
- Bullion wire
- Mirror
- Ribbon
- Stem tape

Method

BOUQUET

1 Before you start making the bouquet, lay out the flowers you need for easy selection as you work. Strip lower leaves from the bracken fronds and cut a 50cm (20in) length of bullion wire ready for tying off the bouquet at the end.

2 Put together an open-centred, airy fan shape, held in your non-dominant hand, using the field pennycress, German statice and bracken fronds – this creates a neutral background structure. At this early stage, consider the shape of the bouquet, checking in a mirror that the structure is even and arranged in an attractive way.

3 Next, using your dominant hand, feed in stems of winged everlasting and sea lavender at the front and back of the bouquet to create a slightly asymmetric spray shape, checking in the mirror as you work.

4 Add some colour and drama with the cornflowers, golden strawflowers, paper daisies, billy buttons and immortelle. The aim at this stage is to create an informal structure that has impact and a sense of movement. Applying these small flowers in loose clusters works well. Either feed a few stems at a time down through the existing structure or add an entire bunch in one go. Make any adjustments to the overall shape of the bouquet by placing an extra stem here and there if needed.

5 With the main structure of the bouquet in place, it's time to add the wow factor with some bold pops of colour in the centre using the dahlias, the and pink and orange strawflowers and the globe thistles. Looking in the mirror as you work, hold up the flowers to see where they will look the best, before gently feeding the stems down through the bouquet. Take your time with this and make sure the flowers can all be seen clearly and have a pleasing overall effect. Add any extra filler flowers in between if needed. Don't worry if it takes a bit of working out to get this right; it's totally normal for a beautiful bouquet to take a bit of time and effort to achieve the desired look.

6 A few final shape enhancers and magic touches of sparkle will complete the look, so use the pink poker statice, wild grasses and shepherd's purse to add a bit of delicate wiggle.

7 Wrap bullion wire around the stems a couple of times and tie securely.

8 Trim the stems to the required length. I have trimmed mine 8–10cm (3–4in) below the bullion wire.

9 For the ultimate flourish, tie a beautiful ribbon or two around the stems.

BUTTONHOLE

1 Firstly, lay out the flowers before stripping off the lower leaves and cutting a 5–10cm (2–4in) length of stem tape to secure the buttonhole with at the end.

2 Using your dominant hand, place first the fern, then the grasses, into your non-dominant hand.

3 Next, place the three sprigs of German statice to the left, the right and the front, and the winged everlasting and billy button at the back.

4 Now tuck the globe thistle, immortelle, strawflower and paper daisy into the front and centre, arranging so that they are all visible and sit well together. Take a moment to check it looks good from all sides, making any adjustments if necessary.

5 Once you are totally happy with how it looks, take the piece of stem tape and wrap it around the stems tightly, just below the flower heads. Decorate with a ribbon of your choice.

6 Trim off unwanted stems to your required length. I have trimmed mine roughly 2cm (¾in) below the ribbon.

TIPS

- If you want a little extra help keeping the flower stems in position during the making process, tie a piece of bullion wire around the stems, leaving enough room to tuck in new stems.
- Creating a well-balanced bouquet like this can take a while, so give yourself plenty of time to enjoy the process.
- To achieve flow in your design, place stems that bend and wiggle to give the illusion of movement.

Starburst Wall Decoration

This design is funky, strikingly simple and radiates joy. I made my first prototype several years ago, and it still hangs on my wall receiving many compliments. I love it when a sunbeam shines through the window onto it, illuminating its golden heart and casting many delicate twiggy shadows. I have used yellow strawflowers here for their dramatic, sunny impact, but you could use any colour you like. This is a robust piece, as the strawflowers hold their colour for years and the twig-and-wire structure is strong and durable.

Perfect for

- Bedrooms
- Chimney breasts or mantels
- Venue décor
- Hallways
- Sitting rooms or lounges
- Kitchens
- Bathrooms
- Doors

Tools & materials

- Tape measure
- Floristry scissors/ secateurs
- 20cm (8in) wire hoop
- Chicken wire, 13mm (½in) gauge holes, 24 x 24cm (9½ x 9½in)
- Wire cutters
- Gloves (optional)
- Binding wire

Flowers & boughs

- 4 x hazel branch, 50cm (20in) long, or equivalent
- 25 x hazel twig, 20–45cm (8–18in) long
- 40–50 x strawflower head, yellow
- 70 x strawflower bud, yellow

Method

SELECT THE HAZEL BRANCHES

1 Decide what overall size you would like your wall decoration to be and select your hazel branches accordingly. This decoration is 1 x 1m (3 x 3ft) at its widest points and the branches are half this size at their longest. Choose nice, branched, balanced pieces that sit as flat as possible.

2 Measure and cut the hazel branches to length with the tape measure and the secateurs. For this example, you will need at least four 50cm (20in); the rest can be 20–45cm (8–18in). Once you have cut the hazel, keep the longest branches in a separate pile ready to use first.

PREPARE THE WIRE FRAME

3 Put the metal hoop on top of a section of chicken wire. Hold it firmly in place, and use your wire cutters to cut around it, allowing an extra 1–2cm (½–1in) to fold over afterwards.

4 Keeping the hoop in place, fold the chicken wire edges around the rim of the wire hoop, taking care to keep it nice and taut as you go. Ensure that you keep the hoop in the centre so that you have enough chicken wire to fold over all the way around. You may want to wear gloves to do this. You should now have a nice, round chicken-wire disc held firmly together.

ATTACH THE HAZEL TWIGS

5 Before you start, cut a handful of 15cm (4in) lengths of binding wire.

6 With the wire disc on a work surface, select the four 50cm (or longest) hazel branches and place them on the disc in a cross shape with the thickest cut ends in the centre butting up against each other. The thinner ends should be facing outwards at 12 o'clock, 3 o'clock, 6 o'clock and 9 o'clock, dividing your emerging starburst into quarters.

Check for shape as you go; all branches are different, and you may want to adjust how they sit in relation to each other to create a pleasing effect.

7 Once you are happy with the position of the longest branches, take a short length of wire and attach each piece of wood twice; once to the outer wire ring and once through the centre of the chicken-wire disc. This should hold them firmly in place. Don't worry too much about how tidy this is as it will be covered in flowers by the end and won't show.

8 Now that you have all four of the longest points of the hazel cross attached, use the hazel twigs to fill the gaps in between them, creating a star effect. Fix them in place as you did the branches.

9 At this point, it's very helpful to attach a small loop of hanging wire to the top branch and hang it on a wall. Stand back and check the shape as you go.

10 Once you have attached all your twigs, stand back and take a look. If you need to, trim any crossing or unwanted side branches to create an even, satisfying effect before you go on to decorate with the flowers.

WIRE ON THE FLOWERS

11 Prepare the strawflowers ready for wiring in place. For the centre I have used large, open strawflowers and for the sides I have used smaller strawflower buds. For each of the large flowers, cut a 20–25cm (8–10in) length of wire, bend it in the middle, then push both ends through the head to create two equal-length wire strands for securing onto the chicken wire (see page 39). For the smaller buds, cut a 10–15cm (4–6in) length of wire and push it through the bud centre to create single strand for securing them to the twigs (see page 39).

12 Starting from the centre, place the larger strawflowers over the chicken-wire disc and twigs ends. They can overlap each other slightly; just make sure they hide the twigs and wire. Thread the wires through to the back of the wire disc and twist to secure.

13 Once the central disc is completely covered with flowers, start to use the smaller flower heads with the single wire strands and attach them directly onto the twigs that fan out from the centre. The flowers should gradually decrease in size and density as they radiate out from the central flower area, enhancing the starburst effect. Keep placing your starburst on the wall so that you can properly view it to check for balance.

14 Lastly, wire a few of the tiniest flower buds carefully along the twigs to the very tips to create a sparkle effect.

TIPS

- Incorporate a few golden dried buttercups and statice into your design for a bit of extra sparkle and texture.
- Make smaller or larger versions of this by using different sized metal hoops in the centre.
- Use any single colour of strawflower to create the look of your choice.

Meadow Flower Panel

This is a unique way of making stunning flower art by creating a meadow in a frame. The fun you can have combining colours and textures in this way is infinite. The effect is fresh, modern and stylish, making a glorious focal point for any space.

For me, there is nothing more enriching than the vibrancy, life and movement that flowers and nature bring to an interior. Flower panels provide the chance to create long-lasting, sustainable interior decoration that evokes wild summer meadows all year round.

Perfect for

- Windows
- Walls
- Weddings
- Shelves or mantels
- Free-standing sculptures
- Bedrooms
- Screens

Tools & equipment

- Cardboard, 40 x 50cm (16 x 20in)
- Tape measure
- Scissors
- Chicken wire, 13mm (½in) gauge holes, 42 x 52cm (16½ x 20½in)
- Gloves (optional)
- Wire cutters
- Floristry scissors/ secateurs
- Binding wire
- Bullion wire

Flowers & boughs

Frame

- 4 x willow stick, 1–1.5cm (¼–½in) thick, or alternative

Base flowers

- 10 x wheat
- 10 x field pennycress
- 10 x bunny tail grass
- 30 x garden and wild grass
- 5 x bracken

Filler flowers

- 10 x larkspur, blue and pink
- 5 x sea holly
- 2–3 x feverfew
- 3 x pink poker statice
- 10 x ageratum, yellow
- 7 x annual statice, white

Show flowers

- 3 x ranunculus
- 20–25 x strawflower, bright
- 5 x African marigold
- 5 x dahlia, orange
- 5 x globe thistle
- 5–10 x paper daisy, pink

Sparkle flowers

- 15 x immortelle
- 5 x cornflower
- 5–7 x billy button
- 10 x paper daisy, white
- 5 x garden and wild grass
- 7 x buttercup

Method

MAKE THE FRAME

1 Measure and cut out a 40 x 50cm (16 x 20in) cardboard template to work from. This can be a flat side of an old cardboard box.

2 Unroll a section of chicken wire and fold it back slightly to flatten it out enough to work with, weighing down the corners with something heavy if it helps. Wire can be very springy and unpredictable with sharp edges, so take care at this stage and wear gloves if you need to.

3 Place your cardboard template over the wire and, using wire cutters, cut around the template approximately 1–2cm (½in) away from the edge. This will allow extra for folding in the sharp wire ends afterwards.

4 Once you have cut all the way around, and while your template is still in place, carefully fold the sharp edges of your chicken wire two thirds of the way inwards over the card to crease your panel edges but so you will still be able to remove the template afterwards. Once this is done, remove the cardboard from the centre and flatten the wire edges the rest of the way down. Check that your wire panel is the correct size by placing the template underneath it. Make any minor adjustments to size at this stage by manipulating the wire, if needed.

5 Choose four willow sticks to go along the top, base and sides of the frame, gently straightening them by hand and bending out any curves. Once you are happy, place them one at a time along the side of your wire-mesh panel, making sure to leave an extra 5cm (2in) at each end for the corners to overlap, then cut off the ends using a pair of secateurs. It is much better to cut your sticks long at this stage; you can always trim them later.

6 Cut 1m (40in) or an arm's length of binding wire and tie or twist one end onto a corner of your wire-mesh panel. Place and hold a willow stick along the side of the mesh, checking that you are happy it's in a good position with an equal length protruding at each end for the corner joins. Start to 'stitch' the willow onto the edge of the mesh panel using the binding wire; do this by going around the stick and through the honeycomb holes along the wire-mesh edge. Keep a firm tension, sewing through every second hole and pulling the wire tight as you go until you reach the other end. Repeat this process on the remaining three sides.

7 Stretch the chicken wire nice and tight before fastening the corners with extra binding wire. Trim any excess off the corner sticks, if necessary, to make them even.

8 Decide which side will be the top of your panel and secure a length of binding wire at the two top corners to create a hanging wire. Your panel is now ready to decorate.

DESIGN THE FLOWER PANEL

9 Consider the design of your flower panel. Think of this as if you are painting a picture with flowers. Your paints are the flowers in all their different colours and textures. Ask yourself how you would like your panel to make you feel when you look at it? Do you want to 'paint' a wildflower meadow or use your favourite colour? Do want it to be busy and full? Bold and vibrant? Or do you visualize something minimal, simple and calm? There is no wrong or right; whatever you decide, enjoy it!

10 'Negative space' areas in your design – areas that are just wire with no flowers – can be a great way to offset the design and make the undulating outline of the top of your panel look natural, delicate and meadow-like. Consider this now, as it will affect the overall look and feel at the end.

11 A helpful order in which you could apply your flowers is: base layer, filler layer, star layer and then sparkle layer. Bear in mind, these are not distinct layers, more like stages that flow from one to the other as you progress. This is only a guideline, but working in this order helps to build up the depth and feel of the design in a way that aids the application of the flowers, which can become trickier as the panel gets more crowded.

ADD THE BASE LAYER

12 Start by weaving in (see pages 40–41) the base layer. In this layer I have used neutral colours, mainly grasses, seed heads or the simpler flowers. This is a great moment to thread in long stems that go all the way from the top to the bottom while you have uninterrupted space to work. Leave a few stems poking up above the top of your frame if you want to. This creates a natural, wild look, as if nature is escaping from the edges of the panel.

ADD THE FILLER LAYER

13 Once you are happy with the base layer, add the filler layer in the same way. This layer provides body, colour and movement to your design. In this part of my design process, I will be looking for a few curved stems, like larkspur, sea holly or similar, to create a weaving effect – just like you might find in nature. Long-stemmed cluster/umbel flowers, randomly spaced at different heights among the grasses, can look wonderful at this stage. I have used feverfew, pink poker statice and ageratum. I like to place some of my flowers in clusters or drifts, as they might grow in the wild, but I will also look for overall balance and a certain amount of symmetry in my design, too, even if it's not obvious at first glance. White annual statice is excellent to use as short stems at the base of the panel. Hold up stems and try them for size in several places to get a feel for placement and compatibility with one another.

14 As you progress with your design, the panel will gradually get busier and more full of stems. It will become fiddlier to find space to thread in new flowers without damaging existing ones. It is totally normal to lose a few flowers at this stage – I do! This is just one of those unavoidable parts of the process, so breathe deeply, take your time and, if you need to, take a break.

15 For short stems or ferns, it is sometimes easier to wire directly onto the panel with bullion wire. Place the wire over the stem, through the chicken wire and tie at the back (see page 41). Tie in any wayward stems that don't wiggle where you want them to or stick out too far with bullion wire.

ADD THE SHOW LAYER

16 Now you have a beautiful background of movement and depth, you can add the pizazz. Time for focal points, colour and all the feature flowers to make an appearance. Get out your strawflowers, dahlias, globe thistles, African marigolds, ranunculi and paper daisies. Decide how bright, how busy and how full you want your design to be. At this stage, consider if you want drifts of colour or randomly spaced spots. Will you choose a theme? Or go crazy with everything? Anything goes – have fun!

ADDING THE SPARKLE LAYER

17 Finally, make your design 'sing' with the sparkle layer. Now is the opportunity to thread any delicate spots of colour and detail to complete the picture. Here I've used star-like purple immortelle, cornflowers, billy buttons and paper daisies to add pops of colour. Fine fronds of delicate grasses or fragile golden buttercups can dance and emerge now that the risk of crushing them in the making is over. Try out a few sparkle flower options to add intense points of light or colour and see what works for you to pull it all together. Finally, add any last-minute strands to escape the panel edges if you like. It's all in the detail.

TIPS

- Try decorating your flower panels in both portrait and landscape orientations; it can achieve some very different, but equally brilliant, effects.
- When designing your panel, consider different styles of flower application. A condensed, central band of flower colour can look very dramatic, top to bottom colour gives maximum coverage or areas of negative space can give a delicate effect and show individual textures beautifully.
- Take out any faded booms and replace them with fresh vibrant flowers as they age over time, or re-use the panel frame, removing the old and replenishing completely with a new design.

Mini Flower Globes

These flowery little orbs are great fun and blow any idea that dried flowers are dull and fusty completely out of the water. They are dazzling and dare to stand out. Hung en masse, they provide a striking, contemporary vibe. Whether it's in a window or above a dining table, these globes are going to be head turners. Make them in any colour you like to create different moods.

Perfect for

- Parties or events
- Windows
- Hallways
- Above tables
- Ceiling decoration
- Stairwells
- Shop and café décor
- Backdrops

Tools & equipment

- Biodegradable floral foam
- Serrated bread knife
- Floristry scissors/ secateurs
- Binding wire
- Bullion wire

Flowers & boughs

- 10 x annual statice per 15cm (6in) globe
- 35 x strawflower per 15cm (6in) globe

Method

1 For the centre of the globe, cut a 6–7cm (2¼–2¾in) square cube of biodegradable floral foam using a serrated bread knife. Trim off the corners to create a rudimentary ball – this doesn't need to be perfect as the flowers will cover it and create the final shape later.

2 To create a wire hanging loop, cut a 70cm (27½in) length of binding wire and fold it in half. Push the folded end through the floral foam until it protrudes out the other side by 5cm (2in) – this will be your hanging loop. Open the loop slightly so that you can hold onto it. Take the other two ends of the wire, bringing one strand up each side of the foam ball, and twist in opposite directions around the base of the hanging loop you've just created. Next, take the two strands back down the remaining opposite sides of the ball to the base, creating a parcel effect, and twist together to secure.

3 Here, I have made a mixture of statice globes and strawflower globes. To prepare the flowers, trim the flower heads to leave short stems of approximately 3–5cm (1–2in) long, cutting at a 45-degree angle to create a pointed stem tip to help push into the foam.

4 Now it's time to decorate! Push the flower stems carefully into your ball (approximately half of the way in), positioning the stems close enough together to hide the foam underneath. As you work, adjust the amount you push the stems in to compensate for any variation in the shape and size of the foam block to achieve a nicely rounded outer finish. Work your way around the globe, adjusting as you go, pulling stems out slightly if you need to.

5 Once you have filled the whole ball, turn it around to check for regularity and fill any gaps. I find gently cupping my hands around the ball and very gently squeezing it can help to hone the curve and create a smoother finished surface.

6 Attach bullion wire to the loop at the top of the flower globe to hang it. Stand back and have another look, making any last-minute minor adjustments to perfect the shape.

TIPS

- Try using fresh flowers to decorate, letting them dry in situ.
- You can use any flowers to decorate your globes, choosing your own beautiful combinations.
- If you don't want to use floral foam, or can't source a biodegradable option, try making a chicken-wire ball with a small amount of moss inside to use instead.

Banquet Table Display

The warm, rich colours and striking textures of this display are like an array of fireworks and make a real statement. It is bold but delicate, with its bright flowers floating above airy stems. It is a stunning way to illuminate any table setting, whatever the occasion. The materials and method are delightfully simple, making this a very enjoyable and rewarding piece to make.

Perfect for

- Tables
- Sideboards
- Shelves or mantels
- Windows
- Celebrations
- Parties and events
- Weddings
- Counter displays

Tools & equipment

- Trough, the one I have used is 80cm (32in) long x 13cm (5in) wide x 8cm (3in) high
- Chicken wire, 13mm (½in) gauge holes, 90 x 50cm (35 x 20in)
- Wire cutters
- Gloves (optional)
- Secateurs/floristry scissors

Flowers & boughs

Base flowers

- 3–4 x birch branch, 1m (40in)
- 2 x hazel branch, 60cm (24in)
- 10–15 x eucalyptus sprigs
- 20 x fern

Show flowers

- 60 x strawflower, orange
- 7 x Chinese lanterns
- 15 x dahlia, red and orange
- 12 x African marigold
- 3 x dill, 50–60cm (20–24in)
- 10 x tansy
- 20 x golden clusters

Sparkle flowers

- 40 x paper daisy, pink
- 10 x cockscomb, pink

Method

PREPARE THE CONTAINER

1 Place the trough on the table it is to be displayed on so that you can work to the scale required.

2 Cut a 90 x 50cm (35 x 20in) section of chicken wire using wire cutters.

3 Taking care of the sharp wire edges (and wearing gloves if necessary), roll and scrunch the chicken wire into a sausage shape that will fit inside your trough, then firmly wedge it in there so that it is level with the top.

DECORATE THE BASE LAYER

4 Cut the birch into 10–40cm (4–16in) lengths with the secateurs and push the ends down into the chicken wire along the length of the trough, making sure to allow plenty to spill out over the sides and ends

5 Place the two hazel branches a quarter of the way in from each end to create extra variation in height.

6 Cut the eucalyptus into 10–30cm (4–12in) lengths and place them evenly between the birch twigs, helping to cover the wire. Once again, make sure the sides and ends look good.

7 Place the ferns at regular intervals along the length to complete the base layer.

DECORATE THE SHOW LAYER

8 Position the orange strawflowers evenly along the centre, sides and ends of the trough. Push them into the chicken wire so they sit at the same level as, or just above, the eucalyptus.

9 Next, add a few clusters of Chinese lanterns at either end of the trough, with a few stems in the centre.

10 Place the dahlias in slightly taller clusters of varying heights around the two hazel branches, so that they appear to float above the display.

11 Position the African marigolds between the dahlias around the hazel, sitting at a height somewhere between the strawflowers and the dahlias. As you work, make sure you check each side, turning the trough so that you look at it from every angle.

12 Add the dill next to the upright hazel branches at either end of the trough.

13 Now that most of the flowers are in place, create clusters of tansy and tuck them between the other flowers to fill any gaps.

14 Lastly, take the golden clusters and use them to fill in around the hazel, between the dahlias and African marigolds, to create a beautiful sparkling effect.

DECORATE THE SPARKLE LAYER

15 Thread in a scattering of bright-pink paper daisies and cockscomb; use longer stems that allow them to float above the other flowers, like a graceful, sparkly haze, completing this beautiful creation. I just love the way a bit of hot pink transforms the other colours, taking them to another level.

TIPS

- Make this in situ so that it is the right size to fit your requirements.
- The trough I have used is made from upcycled pallet wood, which is a great way to make a container any size you want.
- Use moss inside the chicken wire to create an even more stable design (helpful if you need to travel with it).

Summer Flower Crown

Perfect for

- Weddings
- Parties
- Photoshoots
- Fancy dress
- Proms
- Celebrations
- Gifts
- Fashion accessories
- Festivals

Tools & equipment

- Rustic grapevine wire
- Wire cutters
- Secateurs/floristry scissors
- Binding wire
- Ribbon

Flowers & boughs

- 6 x German statice
- 10 x bracken frond
- 10 x bunny tail grass
- 15 x strawflower, gold
- 20 x strawflower, mixed bright colours
- 10 x buttercup
- 15 x immortelle, purple
- 5 x cornflower
- 8 x larkspur, blue
- 1 x peony, pink
- 2 x hydrangea, blue
- 3 x small-leaved eucalyptus

What a joyous thing a crown of colourful flowers is! For centuries they have been used to celebrate the turning of the seasons, the joy of life, important events and special moments. Using everlasting flowers in a crown allows this magic to be enjoyed well beyond the summer months and for much longer than the few hours fresh flowers allow. A crown like this is a real investment, where styles can be explored and glamour created in abundance to be paraded around in time and time again.

Method

PREPARE YOUR MATERIALS

1 Place a length of rustic grapevine wire around your head to work out the right length. You will need to leave a 15cm (6in) gap at the back of your head for the ribbon ties and allow an extra 10cm (4in) on each end of the rustic grapevine wire to double back round to create loops to attach the ribbon to. To make this simple, measuring around your head, plus a bit extra, should work out nicely. When you do this, position the wire as you would like the crown to sit on your head to make sure you measure the right span.

2 Cut the wire to length with the wire cutters, then create a small loop at each end by bending the wire back about 10cm (4in) and twisting it around itself to secure. These loops are where you will attach your ribbon ties later. Bend your crown into a crescent shape and try it on for size, ready for decoration.

3 Lay out your flowers so you can easily reach what you need. I don't cut my stems too short at this stage as it's nice to have varied lengths. However, it is a good idea to reduce them to a manageable size of 15–30cm (6–12in) and divide any bushy stems into smaller pieces.

4 Cut two or three 1m (40in) lengths of binding wire ready to attach the flower stems to the rustic grapevine wire crescent. When one piece runs out, you will have another ready to continue with.

5 Consider the design and shape of the crown. Trying on the crown as you make it, and checking in the mirror as you go, is the best way to get the right shape and look. If you would like the sides of the crown to feather downwards, for example, as mine has, then this early stage is the moment to add some precisely placed stems and bracken.

ADD THE FLOWERS

6 Take two or three stems, such as German statice, bracken and bunny tail grass. Place the stems on the rustic grapevine wire so that the flowers cover the ribbon loops. Wrap the binding wire around the first 2–3cm (1in) of the stems and the rustic grapevine wire a couple of times to hold the stems in place; leave the rest of the wire in position to attach the next set of stems. Trim the remaining ends of the stem with floristry scissors or secateurs.

7 Repeat this process by selecting another three or so stems, perhaps with some colour this time, such as the strawflowers. Lay them along the rustic grapevine wire, overlapping the previous stems slightly, and then wind the binding wire around once or twice again, before repeating with the next flowers.

8 Continue adding stems as above around the crown until you reach the centre. Alternate flowers and foliage to achieve a nice balance. Using clumps of one colour or flower type creates a greater impact. Vary the stem lengths for depth and liveliness. Keep checking for size and shape by trying the crown on.

9 In the centre of the crown, I have used the peony and the hydrangea as a beautiful focal point. Wire these in place in the same way as the other stems.

10 After the midway point in the crown, reverse the direction of the flower's stems as you wire them in place; now the flower heads will be facing down the second side of the crown towards the other loop end. Tuck the cut ends under the large flower heads in step 9 to hide them, then continue wiring as before.

11 I have created a slightly asymmetric style with more flowers on one side, but it's entirely up to you if you do this or keep the flowers the same all the way around. Check that it's still looking okay, and then continue laying and wiring the flowers along the rustic grapevine wire as before.

12 Once you reach the end of the rustic grapevine wire, add a few extra flowers to obscure the loop end. Check in the mirror to see how much it comes down the side of the face and finish as you like.

13 This is the moment to pop in any extra stems to fill gaps and perfect the shape. Do this by carefully pushing additional stems under the existing binding wires. These little details can make all the difference. An extra pop of colour or a bunny tail grass sticking out in the right place can be magic.

14 Cut two 50cm (20in) lengths of ribbon and tie the end of each through the loops at the end of the rustic grapevine wire. Place it on your head and tie snuggly in place with a beautiful bow at the back.

TIPS

- This simple method of making a flower crown can accommodate many different styles. Use the technique above with different stem lengths and colours to achieve a multitude of looks.
- For a less technical option, make a continuous loop of wire to fit around your head, then attach a choice of two or three different flowers in the same direction all the way around.

Vivid Waterfall Mobile

This simple project is easy to make and is a fun way of creating something vibrant and eye-catching for your environment. With semi-translucent flowers and beautiful filigree silhouettes, it will shimmer and glow in stray sunbeams as it moves and spins on a central wire, its colours changing with the light.

Perfect for

- Weddings
- Children's bedrooms
- Hallways or stairwells
- Sitting rooms or lounges
- Windows
- Below skylights or roof lanterns
- Parties or events
- Above tables
- Backdrops or focal points

Tools & equipment

- Tape measure
- Secateurs
- Binding wire
- Chicken wire, 13mm (½in) gauge holes,37 x 37cm (14½ x 14½in)
- Wire cutters
- Bullion wire
- Floristry scissors

Flowers & boughs

- 2 x willow rod, 60cm (24in) long, 10–12mm (½in) thick, or similar
- 10 x Chinese lantern
- 6 x strawflower, orange
- 10 x strawflower, yellow
- 12 x strawflower, red
- 12 x small bracken frond
- 5 x larkspur, pink and blue
- 15 x larkspur 'Blue Cloud'
- 35 x immortelle, purple
- 60 x honesty seed pod
- 3 x African marigold
- 5 x golden cluster
- 20 x hydrangea petal, blue

Method

MAKE THE FRAME

1 Measure the two willow rods with the tape measure and cut them to length with the secateurs. Measure and mark the centre of each rod and then cross the two sticks at this point, securing them together firmly with binding wire.

2 Cut out a square of chicken wire 37 x 37cm (14½ x 14½in) before folding over the ends by 1cm (½in) to remove the sharp edges (reduce this measurement by 1cm/½in if you have an edged side of wire that doesn't need turning in). The overall finished square should be 35 x 35cm (14 x 14in).

3 Place the square of chicken wire over the centre of the willow cross so that each corner sits on a rod. This should leave approximately 6cm (2½in) of rod protruding beyond each corner. Once you are happy with the position of the square fix it to the cross by attaching them together with binding wire. Attach the centre first, then fasten each corner of the chicken wire to the ends of the willow rods, pulling it taut as you go.

4 To make hanging wires, cut four 60cm (24in) lengths of binding wire. Tie the end of each one around a willow rod at the point where the chicken wire ends. Bring each strand of wire to a central point and hold it up to check the frame is level. Twist all four wires together before looping it back round to create a central loop to hang the mobile from.

5 Hang the mobile frame from a central wire, fixed through the wire hoop. Hang it at a comfortable working height, just above head, so you can easily reach it and so you can see how it looks as you work. Check that the square frame is horizontally level from every angle and make any adjustments by tweaking the wire if required.

ADD THE DECORATION

6 Time to make the beautiful flower strands! Each one is made by wiring flower heads to a length of bullion wire at 5–10cm (2–4in) intervals (see page 40) before hanging them from the chicken-wire frame. In my mobile, I have used approximately 40 strands of wire of varying lengths, from 5cm (2in) to 80cm (32in). Some have multiple flowers, while others have single flowers with stems and leaves. The idea is to create a random mixture of colours and textures at all levels so it looks beautiful from every angle. I have made mine fuller and thicker at the top, feathering gradually down to the bottom.

7 Once you have made the flower strands, hang them from the frame by twisting the end of the bullion wire around the mesh. Start from the centre and work outwards as you go. Remember, this mobile will turn and spin round gently on its central wire, so make sure you work on every side, checking it looks great from all directions. It's good to play with the colours and textures, trying out combinations until you are happy with the way they sit together to create an elegant, colourful waterfall.

TIPS

- To use this as a stunning, full-length backdrop, increase the length of the flower strands.
- Try using fresh flowers, letting them dry in situ.
- Make this project with children. You can use a few foraged leaves and flowers, too.

Strawflower Streamers

These colourful ribbons of flowers shout joy! They are so simple to make and only need a very simple set of tools and materials to create. They show off the vibrant flower colours beautifully and are suitable for many locations and occasions – you could even wear them! Throughout history, people have celebrated and enjoyed flowers in this way across the world, and you can see why. It may be an ancient idea, but it still looks contemporary and exciting to this day.

Perfect for

- Parties
- Weddings
- Events
- Bedrooms
- Hallways and landings
- Celebrations
- Kitchens
- Sitting rooms or lounges
- Shop or café décor
- Windows
- Christmas decorations
- Christmas tree décor

Tools & equipment

- Floristry scissors/secateurs
- Tape measure
- Jute garden twine
- Large needle (e.g. wool or darning needle)

Flowers & boughs

- 15–20 x strawflower head per 1m (40in)

Method

1 Prepare the flowers by trimming off any stems with the floristry scissors and placing them close to hand. The flowers can vary in size and colour; I've used individual colours on each strand here, but they can look equally good mixed together in different combinations.

2 Measure your required length of jute twine, allowing an extra 30cm (12in) on each end for securing, and thread one end onto the needle.

3 Push the threaded needle through the centre of a flower and slide it all the way to the far end of the twine, leaving the last 30cm (12in) of twine for tying later. Tie a simple knot in the twine between each flower to ensure they stay nicely spaced. You will find the slightly rough, hairy nature of the jute twine will help to keep the flowers in position, too.

4 Repeat this process, keeping each flower facing the same way, spacing them at 5–10cm (2–4in) intervals. This may feel a bit slow to start with, but it soon speeds up as you start adding flowers.

5 When you have finished adding flowers to your strand, either tie loops at the end of the twine to hang the streamer from or simply tie the twine to a fixing point, and enjoy!

TIPS

- Many other flowers would look amazing used in this way. Have fun trying out different combinations and colour schemes.
- If you decide a streamer isn't long enough, just tie on another length of twine and add more flowers.
- This is an ideal activity to do with children and friends.

2

PASTELS

Blossom Branch

Perfect for

- Tables (in single vases or bottles)
- Tables (in multiple vases)
- Sideboards, mantels or shelves
- Walls
- Doorways or windows
- Free-standing sculptures

Tools & equipment

- Secateurs/floristry scissors
- Binding wire
- Heavy based vase or container to hold the branch upright while you work

Flowers & boughs

- 1 x hazel or birch branch, 45–50cm (18–20in) long, or similar
- 25–30 x strawflower in varying sizes and colours of your choice

To me, blossom is a vision of joy and hope. It signals the beginning of new life and fruits to come. The way the blossoms appear along often naked, leafless branches only makes the delicate flowers stand out even more exquisitely. Creating your own sculptural version of blossom is a simple but stunning way to capture that ethereal beauty; but rather than just a fleeting spring display, this will continue to give delight all year round. You can make blossom branches to any scale you want, from tiny tabletop twigs right up to the size of a tree! They create a big impact, with comparatively little effort and minimal materials.

Method

SELECT YOUR MATERIALS

1 One of the most important things is to find the right branch for the job. Look for a branch with character and well-spaced, open, fine-tipped twigs. Hazel and birch are both great for this, but any similar finely structured tree or shrub will do. The aim is for it to look good from any angle and have a pleasing overall shape.

2 Select your flowers. I have used strawflowers of varying sizes, in shades of pink, salmon, cream and pale yellow to give a subtle variation in tone as you often see in nature.

You can use flowers with or without stems. There are advantages to both options and I often use a combination of the two. Flowers with stems can be wired directly onto the branch, which is the quickest way of attaching them. However, the flowers can snap off easily and the flower angles can look haphazard. Using individual flower heads by wiring in a 'fake' stem is fiddlier to prepare initially, but has the advantage of allowing you to angle the flower in any direction without them breaking. It's also a wonderful way to use up all those loose, left-over flower heads that you may have from other projects.

ADD THE FLOWERS

3 Use the secateurs to cut stemmed flowers to a length of approximately 10cm (4in).

To create a wire stem for a strawflower head, cut a 15cm (6in) length of binding wire. Carefully poke one end of the wire through the outer edge of the flower centre – taking care to keep fingertips out of the way underneath – and pull it two-thirds of the way through. Push the other end of the wire through the flower centre, 0.5cm (¼in) away from the initial wire, and gently pull through, creating a loop effect on the flower head. Turn the flower over and firmly twist the two wires together on the back, creating a wire stem.

4 Before you attach your flowers, place your branch in a vase or container to hold it upright while you are working on it. (You can wedge a cloth in to hold it steady if that helps.)

APPLY THE FLOWERS

5 To attach a stemmed flower, cut a 10cm (4in) length of binding wire. Place your flower so the head comes away from the branch or beyond the twig tip and the stem runs flat along the twig. Tightly wrap the wire around the flower stem and the twig several times, keeping it as neat as possible. Take care not to snap the twig or the flower stem at this point, which can happen very easily! It is fiddly work, so don't rush.

To attach a pre-wired flower head, wind the bottom half of your wire tightly around the twig several times and as neatly as possible, allowing enough wire underneath the flower head to manoeuvre it into a good position.

6 Continue to work your way through the twigs, carefully attaching your flowers. Turn the branch as you go to make sure the flowers are evenly spaced and your display looks great from all angles. There's no need to fill every single twig, just keep going until you feel happy with its overall look.

7 At the end, fill any odd gaps and tweak flowers into position to perfect your branch.

TIPS

- Using small strawflower buds at the very tips of the branches and larger open flowers further down can help give the impression of emerging blossom buds in spring.
- Other flowers can work well for decorating branches, such as honesty, hydrangeas, immortelle and paper daisies, to name a few.
- Blossom branches are light and easy to send in the post, so make a lovely gift.

Pastel Garland

Garlands have a rich history. They have been used by many cultures all over the world. They have been enjoyed as symbols of love, the arrival of spring, eternal life, beauty, good luck, welcome, celebration and ceremony. They have brought decoration to weddings, banquets, social gatherings, buildings and objects of special importance for thousands of years. These flowers provide beauty, joy and celebration; what a fabulous feeling to weave into any creation.

The movement and flexibility of a garland is brilliant to work with, allowing it to curl or flow over and around things. They can work well where wall space is limited, fitting in along a cupboard top, mantel or over a mirror or picture frame, giving an injection of natural wilderness. They also work wonderfully in grander locations, such as archways, events and weddings, where they conjure up a feeling of opulence, abundance and frivolity.

Perfect for

- Doorways, arches or windows
- Banisters
- Tables
- Mantels or above fireplaces
- Cupboards
- Mirrors or picture frames
- Shelves
- In swags, just about anywhere

Tools & equipment

- Tape measure
- Thick jute rope or, alternatively, anything flexible bound together – for example, pairs of old tights, reused strips of fabric or dried grass or straw
- Secateurs/floristry scissors
- Binding wire, alternatively string or raffia may be used
- Wire cutters

Flowers & boughs

Show flowers

- 50–60 x strawflower, pastel
- 2 x bunch winged everlasting
- 2 x bunch immortelle, purple
- 10–15 x billy button
- 5–6 x hydrangea

Filler flowers

- 2–3 x honesty
- 1 x bunch lady's mantle
- 1 x bunch bunny tail grass
- 1 x bunch shepherd's purse

Foliage

- 10 x traveller's joy
- 20 x bracken
- 1 x bunch birch twigs
- 25 x sprigs eucalyptus or box

Method

MAKE THE BASE

1 Decide where your garland is going to be situated. What length does it need to be? How bushy do you want it? Is its width important for where it's going to sit? What colours might complement its surroundings? Use a tape measure to help you.

2 To form your base, lay out three or four lengths of rope, cutting them 20cm (6–8in) or so shorter than your finished garland to allow room for the flowers to feather over and conceal the rope ends.

3 To assemble your base, gather the lengths of rope together and attach the end of the binding wire around one end of the of the bunch of rope strands. Then, keeping the reel of wire in one hand while holding the bunch of ropes in the other, wind the wire around the entire length of the ropes, every 1cm (½in) or so, and secure. This will create a nice firm but pliable base to attach to.

PREPARE THE POSIES

4 Decide which flowers, colours and textures you would like to use and gather them together. It's helpful to have them all laid out and close to hand, as once you get into the flow you don't want to have to keep stopping to get more materials.

5 The next stage is to make a series of little individual posies of foliage and flowers that will be wired along the length of your rope base, combining to create your beautiful finished design. The size and tightness of your posies will determine the width of the garland and how neat or how bushy it will turn out. To give you an idea, a 10–15cm (4–6in) posy will result in a 20–30cm (8–12in) garland width.

To make the posies, select a mixture of five or six different elements, including twigs (if you're using them), a filler or two, a couple of grasses and one or two flower options. As a rough guide, I tend to use about one-third show flowers to two-thirds foliage and fillers. Once you have a nice, small posy in your hand, make sure it's evenly spread out and not too bunched up, then wrap a piece of binding wire around the stems to secure, trimming any excess off afterwards. The bunches don't need to all be the same; you can alternate the ingredients of each one individually so long as you repeat and distribute the different flowers and textures along the length of the garland to give an even effect. You can either make a few at a time or make them as you construct your garland.

7 At the other end of the rope, position the last couple of posies so that they change direction, tucking the stem ends in and allowing the flowery end to feather out beyond the rope, hiding it nicely to finish off.

8 Check for any gaps where the rope is visible or places lacking in colour or balance. You can either tie in an extra little posy here and there or gently tease individual stems into existing posies.

9 Check the finished overall look. Does it need any extra pinpricks of colour to really make it sing? Now is the time to tuck in a few bright or even clashing points of colour. I've used some acid-yellow billy buttons to give mine an edge and tucked in a few orange strawflowers to lift an otherwise muted pink palette.

ATTACH THE POSIES

6 Lay your rope base flat on your work surface, then lay your first posy over it so that the feathery flowery end sticks out beyond the rope base by 10cm (4in) or so – you don't want to be able to see the end of the rope. Firmly fix the posy in position using a piece of binding wire by wrapping it around the rope a couple of times and securing it. Lay the second mini posy in the same direction as the first, overlapping it by about half of the previous one, and wire in place so you can't see the previous bunch's stem ends. Repeat this process along the rope base, staggering your posies so the rope is not visible and you have nice and balanced colour and texture. This can feel fiddly to start with but stick with it; it will come together.

TIPS

- Play with style! Use extra birch twigs, bracken or seed heads for a wild, natural look with lots of movement, which looks great where you have the space. For a compact, colourful option, reduce your filler flowers and increase your show flowers to create something intense and dazzling.
- Think about where the garland will be positioned and what sides will be visible, then plan your most colourful side to face that way. This can save time and avoid using flowers where they won't be seen, such as against the wall along the back of a mantelpiece.

Spring Bouquet

A bouquet packed with everlasting flowers in gentle, soft colours is a joy to behold. It brings movement and emotion with its textures and subtle colours – and does not require water or light. Whether for a home, wedding or gift, this is an incredibly versatile and long-lasting display for any occasion.

Perfect for

- Table centrepieces
- Sideboards, mantels or shelves
- Gifts
- Weddings
- In disused fireplaces
- Small display tables or pedestals

Tools & equipment

- Bullion wire
- Floristry scissors/ secateurs
- Ribbon (optional)
- Vase or jug (optional)

Flowers & Boughs

Foliage

- 7 x eucalyptus

Filler flowers

- 5 x field pennycress
- 5 x feverfew
- 5 x gypsophila
- 10 x annual statice, pastel
- 5 x astrantia, pink
- 5 x aquilegia seed head
- 10 x larkspur; pink and pale blue
- 4–5 x hydrangea

Grasses

- 20 x wild foraged grasses
- 10 x bunny tail grass
- 10 x wild foxtail millet grass

Show flowers

- 10 x dahlia, pink
- 10 x cornflower, mauve
- 5 x chrysanthemum, yellow
- 30 x strawflower, pastel
- 25 x paper daisy, pink

Method

1 To achieve a well-balanced bouquet with depth and movement, you will need a selection of filler flowers, foliage and grasses to bring lightness to the design, to bring volume to the arrangement and to display the show flowers at their best.

Lay out the flowers into easily accessible piles. Prepare your flower stems by stripping off any dead leaves or unwanted side branches and dividing any larger stems into smaller, more manageable pieces.

2 Cut a 50cm (20in) length of bullion wire ready for tying off the bouquet at the end. This wire is great for tying up a finished bouquet as the crimped wire grips the stems, holding them securely in place.

3 Select five filler stems to start with, such as field pennycress or feverfew, as well as some of the grasses. Cross the stems midway down so they splay out both top and bottom. You will be creating a spiral of stems and where they cross will be the centre. To help get a spoked effect from the beginning, hold the crossing point in the middle with your thumb and the lower stem ends between your fingers of the same hand to keep them separated. Use a piece of wire to loosely secure the stems at any point if it helps.

4 Using your free hand, start to add new stems, laying them diagonally, following the crossed angle of the existing stems. While holding them in place with your thumb, carefully turn the bouquet 2–3cm (1–2 in) at a time, adding more stems as you go to build up the spiral. This stage can be fiddly to start with, so take your time. Hold the stems loosely, so that the bouquet remains nice and open at the top and bottom, but firmly enough so that it does not twist out of shape.

5 Continue adding flowers to the centre of the bouquet. As you add flowers, think about the distribution of the different elements, making sure that you include a mix of grasses, fillers and show flowers. Sometimes I like to add several stems at once, for example, four or five stems of varying lengths, to create an asymmetric spray effect that adds to the feeling of movement.

6 You may find as you build up the spiral that some stems slip down; this is quite normal, if a little irritating. Just keep an eye on it and gently pull them back up into place.

7 As you turn your bouquet, check for gaps that may have opened as you've been working, placing in extra flowers to fill them. The beauty of these flowers not needing water is you can pop in some shorter stems once you've got a structure to hold them in place. It really doesn't matter if they don't go all the way to the bottom so long as they are secure.

8 Before the bouquet gets too big to hold in your hand, add a few stems lower down on the sides, creating a slightly rounded-off effect. It's nice to include a few curved stems that spread out sideways and provide balance and movement to the finished bouquet.

9 When you think you are finished, turn the bouquet around a few times, checking for gaps and balance, and adding more flowers where necessary. Once you are happy, get a length of bullion wire, approximately 50cm (20in), and wrap it around the middle of the stems twice, pulling it tight, gently but firmly, and twisting several times to secure.

10 Trim the stems to the required length with floristry scissors. If the bouquet is to go in a vase, measure it up against the vase before cutting. I recommend cutting slightly long to start with, allowing room for trimming afterwards. Better to have too much than too little! For my bouquet, I have cut the stems approximately 15cm (6in) bellow the wire in the middle, which is a nice length for a free-standing bouquet or vase. Once you have completed this, you may need to tease the stems apart a bit to re-establish the spoked effect and open the bouquet head up again to regain its shape.

11 Tie ribbon or string to cover the securing wire around the stems. Then stand back and admire your handiwork!

TIPS

- Once you have securely tied your bouquet and trimmed your stems, stand it up, step back and turn it all the way around a few times to view from every angle. If it needs a few more flowers here and there, carefully push the stems down into the securing wire until you are entirely happy with it.
- Add a few longer stems or even a few twigs at the end to really enhance the asymmetric effect and make it extra special.
- If you want a few distinctive sprays of one type of flower at varying hights in your bouquet, wire a few stems together at their base with bullion wire beforehand. This will make it easier to apply them when your hands are full in the middle of construction.
- This is quite a large bouquet, but it can be made smaller with fewer flowers or a simpler flower palette.

Heart Flower Panel

I love making heart-shaped flower panels as they radiate love in every respect. From the delicate outline of the frame to the soft colours and textures of the flowers, they're enough to melt anyone's heart. There are so many ways to play with the decoration and size of this lovely shape, making each one a unique treasure.

Perfect for

- Children's nurseries or bedrooms
- Weddings
- Sitting rooms or lounges
- Shelves or mantels
- Parties or events
- Stairways, landings or hallways
- Kitchens
- Windows
- Bedrooms
- Doors

Tools & equipment

- Cardboard, 50 x 50cm (20 x 20in)
- Marker pen
- Scissors
- Chicken wire, 13mm (½in) gauge holes, 52 x 52cm (20½ x 20½in)
- Gloves (optional)
- Wire cutters
- Tape measure
- Binding wire
- Floristry scissors/ secateurs
- Bullion wire

Flowers & boughs

- 2 x willow rod, 1.5m (5ft) long, 8–10mm (¼–½in) thick

Base flowers

- 15 x wild grass
- 6 x achillea 'The Pearl'
- 6 x bladder campion

Filler flowers

- 5 larkspur, pale blue
- 5 annual statice, white
- 5 annual statice, yellow

Show flowers

- 8 x ranunculus, pastel
- 12 x paper daisy, pink
- 6 x cornflower, white
- 6 x cornflower, pastel blue
- 7 x bistort, pale pink
- 4 x strawflower head, pale yellow
- 4 x strawflower head, pale pink
- 6 x bunny tail grass

Sparkle flowers

- 10 x immortelle, purple
- 6 x buttercup

Method

MAKE THE FRAME

1 To make your template, place the sheet of cardboard on a flat work surface. Using a marker pen, draw a heart outline before cutting around it with scissors. The one I have made here is roughly 50 x 50cm (20 x 20in).

2 Unroll a section of chicken wire and fold it back slightly to flatten it out enough to work with (weigh down the corners with something heavy if it helps). Wire can be very springy and unpredictable, with sharp edges, so take care at this stage and wear gloves if you need to.

3 Place your cardboard template over the wire, hold it down firmly and use the wire cutters to cut around the heart 1–2cm (½in) from the template edge. This will allow extra for folding in the sharp sides afterwards.

4 Once you have cut all the way around – and while your template is still in place – carefully fold the wire inwards by two-thirds, all the way along edge, to crease it along the sides. Then remove the cardboard and push the wire down until it is flat. Check that your wire panel is the correct shape by placing the template underneath it, making any minor adjustments by manipulating the wire into position if needed. Due to the nature of the chicken-wire structure, it is normal to have a slightly wonky edge in the places where it curves.

5 Select two 1.5m (5ft) willow rods. The thick ends will be used at the base of the heart so that the thinner, more flexible ends can be curved around the top and into the centre. They will need a bit of 'flexing' to take on a nice curve: using the template as a guide, hold a willow rod with two hands and gently but firmly press outwards, using both of your thumbs, every 3–4cm (2–3in). Continue doing this along the length of the rod to gently encourage the willow to stretch into shape and become more pliable. Repeat with the second rod. Don't worry if you break one or two, sometimes it takes a couple of goes to get it right.

6 To stitch the frame and wire together, cut an arm's length of binding wire and attach it to the first of your willow rods.

7 Place the willow around your chicken-wire heart and 'stitch' it onto the edge of the mesh using the binding wire. Do this by wrapping it around the willow and threading it through the honeycomb holes along the wire-mesh edge. Keep a firm tension, sewing through every second hole and pulling the wire tight as you go until you have gone all the way around. This can be a little fiddly as you curve around the top and bend the willow into shape, so take your time. Repeat the process with the second rod to complete your shape.

8 Check the frame against the template again and pull it into its final shape. Use binding wire to securely fix the crossing points at the top and bottom of the frame by wrapping wire tightly around them. Trim off any excess willow or binding wire for a tidy finish.

9 Tie a length of binding wire at the top of your heart to hang it from.

DECORATE THE BASE LAYER

10 Before you start, take a moment to consider the layout of the design. Ask yourself how much of the space you want to fill. Leaving a small area at the top of the design empty can allow the outline of the grasses and small flowers to be appreciated and helps to give a sense of delicacy. Curving the flowers to follow the shape of the frame can look great, with a few escaping fronds to add a sense of movement.

11 Working either on a wall or at a table, start by adding the longest stems, such as the wild grasses. Hold each one up to see how it looks before threading the stem down through the chicken wire, weaving it in and out to fix it firmly in place (see pages 40–41).

12 Place different flowers and grasses in clumps to create a stronger impact and emulate the plant drifts found in nature.

DECORATE THE FILLER LAYER

13 Continue adding flowers in the same way as the grasses. Use the larkspur to start filling the gaps and to build texture, layering them over the grass stems in beautiful flowing lines. Shorter pieces of yellow and white statice can be used to fill the bottom triangle of the heart and curve up around the sides. Use bullion wire for extra support to get them to follow the shape you want and to fix them in position if needed (see pages 40–41).

DECORATE THE SHOW LAYER

14 The ranunculi are the showstoppers of the showy layer, so position them centre stage. Add the pink paper daisies in drifts in between the other flowers up one side of the heart and the pale blue cornflowers up the other.

15 The pink bistort looks great popping up at the top, while the other flowers, such as the strawflowers and bunny tails, can be used to fill in any gaps and balance the design.

DECORATE THE SPARKLE LAYER

16 Add the little star-shaped immortelles drifting up between the ranunculi; the little pop of purple really sets the design off.

17 Finally, add a few delicate clumps of sparkly yellow buttercups to lift all the colours and finish the design beautifully.

TIPS

- If dried flowers are tricky to source, see what meadow flowers and grasses you can find near you, then buy a few fresh flowers, like roses, statice and ranunculi, to dry and use in your flower heart.
- To save time, use a pre-made heart-shaped frame instead of making one from willow.
- Find a natural curve in flower stems to follow the outline of the heart shape.

Easter Wreath

A floral wreath or ring of flowers is a centuries-old form of floral decoration. As well as a rich history, this wreath also has it has roots in the ever-turning cycle of life, of birth and death and the renewing of hope. This wreath has a fresh, modern feel that makes it an exciting piece of contemporary art. It enriches any space and brings a room alive with its presence. Wreaths are wonderful for providing year-round enjoyment as interior decoration.

Perfect for

- Walls
- Above fireplaces
- Around mirrors
- Table centrepieces
- Doors
- Windows
- Bedrooms

Tools & equipment

- Binding wire
- Wire cutters
- Tape measure
- Floristry scissors/ secateurs

Flowers & boughs

Boughs

- 50–100 x willow rod, 0.5cm (¼in) thick, or similar flexible stems
- 50 x birch twig, 10–40cm (4–15in) long
- 3–5 x hop bine, 1m (3ft) long, or similar climbing plant

Base flowers

- 20 x field pennycress
- 10 x feverfew
- 10 x German statice
- 10 x annual statice, white
- 10 x annual statice, pastel
- 10 x short stems honesty
- 20 x catmint
- 20 x winged everlasting

Show flowers

- 70–80 x strawflower, pastel
- 8 x globe thistle
- 30 x paper daisy, pink and white
- 10 x annual statice, yellow

Sparkle flowers

- 10 x winged everlasting
- 10 x cornflower, pale blue
- 10 x shepherd's purse

Method

MAKE THE RING

1 The base ring is – in effect – a long, thin sausage made of willow sticks, bound together and bent round before being wired in place to form a circle. To make the ring, select two or three willow rods and place the cut ends together. Secure them near the ends with binding wire, keeping the reel of wire attached.

2 Holding the willow and the reel of wire in your non-dominant hand, pick up one or two more willow rods with your dominant hand, placing them at staggered intervals along the existing willow, working away from the cut ends. Wrap wire around the willow twice, at intervals of 2–3cm (¾–1in), to hold the new rods in place, keeping a firm but not tight wire tension. It's important not to bind it together too tightly, as you will need to be able to thread your flower stems under the wire in between the rods later.

3 Repeat this process with one or two new rods, moving along as you go to create a willow sausage. Repeat until it is 3–4cm (1–1½in) thick, and you have bound a length of approximately 130cm (51in), leaving the remaining willow ends unbound at this stage.

4 Taking the end that you started with firmly in your non-dominant hand and the feathery end in the other, bend the cut ends round and tuck into the inside side of your sausage. There can be quite a bit of tension in the bound willow at this stage, so be prepared to use a bit of muscle! The cut willow ends should roughly match up with where you have wired to.

5 Bend the feathery, thinner ends round the outside of your loop, hopefully creating an even thickness by overlapping the two tapered ends and forming a nice circle. Hold the ends together with your non-dominant hand and measure for size with the tape measure. You can release the tension slightly and slide the ends in or out to adjust the size slightly if needed. If it's not big enough, release and add more willow.

6 Once you are happy with the size, continue to wrap the wire around the combined willow rods until all the ends are bound and secure, remembering not to bind it too tightly, then tie or twist the wire to complete.

7 Check the shape of your ring. It may need a bit of help bending into a circle. Using your knee to gently push out from the inside can help with this.

8 Wrap extra wire around your ring to fix the flowers onto during the decorating process. Take the reel of wire, attach it to the ring, then wind it every 1cm (½in) right the way around the ring. Cut and secure.

9 Attach a 15cm (6in) loop of wire at the top of the willow ring to use for hanging.

ADD THE BACKGROUND STRUCTURE

10 This is the moment you can decide just how wild and wayward you would like your design to be. If you want a neat effect, cut your birch twigs short and regular; if you want a wild and free feel, cut them long and irregular. Where you cut the birch will also depend on the branch itself. Use the secateurs to cut the birch to your required length, ranging from 10–40cm (4–16in). Cut them at an angle to create points that will slide under the wires easily. It is worth taking your time on this process, as it sets the architectural structure of the background of the wreath.

11 You can work on your wreath on a tabletop or while hanging on a wall – whichever option is easiest or preferable to you. I make mine on a wall as I like to stand back and see it from all angles as I make it.

12 Push the cut birch ends under the willow ring wires, wedging them in between the willow rods until you can feel them grip securely in place. It may take a couple attempts to find the right place. I tend to choose and stick to a direction to work in to create an informal wheel effect that has a sense of movement to it.

13 Continue adding the birch around the outside and inside the edges of the ring with varying lengths of twig until you have an even, well-structured effect.

ADD THE BACKGROUND LAYER

14 Building up the filler background layers is where the main body of the wreath is created. Cut varied lengths 10–20cm (4–8in) of field pennycress. Following the same angle and direction as the birch, push the stem ends under the ring wires in between the birch, making sure they are lodged firmly in place. Space them at irregular 10–20cm (4–8in) intervals. Add a few smaller bits to the front and inner edge.

15 Repeat this process with the feverfew, statice and honesty, varying the lengths and spacings to help give a sense of movement and depth to the design.

16 Cut the catmint and winged everlasting a little longer – to lengths of 20–30cm (8–12in). Then add them to the ring, as above, making sure to place some of the longer stems at the back.

17 If you are working on a tabletop, get someone to hold the wreath up at this stage so you can stand back and check its shape from a distance and adjust if necessary.

ADD THE SHOW LAYER

18 The main focus of the show layer is a jostling array of strawflowers in stunning shades of pink, apricot, lemon yellow, white, cream and many tones in between. I pre-wire all my strawflowers as it allows me to bend the heads in any direction, helping to achieve a natural feel and eliminating the risk of flower heads snapping off. You can use flowers on a stem or a combination of wired and non-wired flowers, depending on how you feel. Wire your strawflowers (see page 39), if you wish to do so.

19 Cut the stems of the globe thistles at an angle so that the sharp point will slide under the wires easily. Place them evenly around the wreath where they will show up well at the front. Push the stems under the willow ring wires until they grip firmly in place.

20 Place the strawflowers between the globe thistles. Hold up the different colours as you work to see which colour combinations go well together. Push them into place. Place a few flowers with slightly longer stems around the sides, too.

21 Once you have built up a nice, even layer of strawflowers, you can add the pink and white paper daisies and lemon yellow statice in between them. Put a few around the sides, filling all the gaps.

22 Once again, stand back and view your wreath form a distance to check the overall shape for balance and colour, adding the odd extra stem where needed.

ADD THE SPARKLE LAYER

23 For the final finishing touches, add a sprinkling of white winged everlasting and pastel-blue cornflowers for a bit of contrast and a few strands of shepherd's purse scattered throughout for its wiggly effect and gorgeous silhouettes.

24 Tuck and weave a few strands of dried hop bine or similar climbing plant around the back of the wreath, wiring to the willow base in a few places to secure. This adds a little touch of wilderness that I love.

TIPS

- At all stages of decorating, check how the wreath looks from the side, making sure to add flowers at the back and sides so that it looks great from every angle.
- At the end of decorating your wreath, try hanging it on a wall and stand back to look at the overall shape and outline. Tuck in a few longer strands of birch at the back and sides, if needed, to give it balance.
- When adding the strawflowers, place them more densely in the centre of the ring, gradually reducing the amount as you move further out.

Romantic Pedestal

This heart-stopping design manages to capture the essence of delicate meadow flowers and scented rambling hedgerows in its wayward, wild nature. The luxurious roses and the arrangement's pastel palette make it wildly romantic and is sure to get the flower lover's pulse racing. The time taken to carefully place each stem with love and attention is as rewarding as gazing upon it afterwards.

Perfect for

- Side tables
- Mantels or shelves
- Table displays
- Parties or events
- Business receptions
- Weddings
- Shop or café décor
- Focal points
- Hallways

Tools & equipment

- Chicken wire, 13mm (½in) gauge holes, 30 x 30cm (12 x 12in)
- Wire cutters
- Gloves (optional)
- Footed flower bowl, 14cm (5½in) wide and 13cm (5in) high
- Pot tape
- Floristry scissors/ secateurs

Flowers & boughs

- 10 x eucalyptus
- 2 x hydrangea, pink
- 10 x larkspur, pastel
- 3 x achillea, pink
- 2 x meadow rue
- 5 x Queen Anne's lace
- 10 x roses, pastel
- 2 x peony, white
- 10 x strawflower, pastel
- 10 x ranunculus, pastel
- 15 x wild grasses
- 10 x bistort, pink
- 3 x shepherd's purse

Method

PREPARE THE FOOTED BOWL

1 Cut out a 30 x 30cm (12 x 12in) square of chicken wire using the wire cutters or use a similar sized offcut if you have one.

2 Scrumple the chicken wire into a ball and place it in the footed bowl. The footed bowl I have used is 14cm (5½in) wide and 13cm (5in) high. The ball should fit neatly inside and be flush with the top. Take care of sharp wire ends and wear gloves if you need to.

3 Tape the chicken wire ball down using two pieces of pot tape; place them in a cross shape over the bowl with 4–5cm (1–2in) down each side to hold it firmly in place.

DECORATE

4 The first step of the decoration is to establish the shape and outline of your asymmetric design using the eucalyptus. I have made one side taller and curving inwards slightly, while the other side curves downwards to the opposite side. Push each stem firmly into the chicken wire ball, so they feel secure in place. Make sure to add a few smaller bits spraying out around the front and sides, too. This creates a nice open centre for the flowers and beautiful movement and drama.

5 Place the two hydrangea heads slightly off-centre at the front; this helps hide the wire and should leave enough space for other flowers later. Take your time finding the shape; it can take a few goes, but it's worth establishing now to build the rest of the design on.

6 Start adding filler flowers – the larkspur, achillea, meadow rue and Queen Anne's lace – to build up the structure and bring in some background colour. Place these to enhance the background look of the eucalyptus and hydrangea, and to help hide the chicken wire and pot tape. Try and keep the centre of the design open so there is space for the next layer of flowers.

7 Now it's time to put in some glitz and glamour. Start with the shortest stems first. I used the roses, peonies and strawflowers in the centre of the design, radiating out to complement the existing background shape. You can always do a bit of adjusting later as well. Stand back to check how it looks from a distance every now and then.

8 Start to add a few longer stems alongside the taller eucalyptus – here, I have used the ranunculi. Hold each stem up and try it for size in different positions before finally placing it. These spots of colour make a big difference to how the eye is drawn to the shape; the subtle placement or the twist of a stem can have a huge impact.

9 Now for the final magical stems to bring it all together. Use the wild grasses and bistort to fill any gaps, enhance the shape, and add delicacy and movement. Again, stand back to check how it looks and take the time to make any small adjustments. This is art after all! Finally, pop in the shepherd's purse stems for the last bit of detail to bring it to completion.

TIPS

- Some of the flowers in this design may be available in a flower shop or supermarket, or could be foraged. It can be fun to collect your own selection of flowers to dry and use.
- It can be helpful to make a design like this in situ so that you can tailor the shape to suit the space, lighting and orientation.

Rustic Wall Sculpture

This dramatic wall sculpture design is a brilliant combination of organic, rustic form and flowery romance. The frame of twisted, characterful branches makes each one totally unique and is a striking contrast to the sugary-sweet pastel flowers used in its decoration. The free-form approach to creating this piece makes it a great project to enjoy letting your creativity run wild.

Perfect for

- Above fireplaces
- Hallways or landings
- Focal points
- Bedrooms
- Weddings
- Shop or café décor
- Stairwells
- Sitting rooms or lounges
- Kitchens
- Doors

Tools & equipment

- Binding wire
- Secateurs
- Chicken wire, 13mm (½in) gauge holes
- Wire cutters
- Gloves (optional)
- Floristry scissors/ secateurs
- Bullion wire

Flowers & boughs

Frame

- 2–3 characterful branches that have a naturally bowed or angular shape; I have used 2 x ivy branches, 1m (39in) long

Base flowers

- 25–30 x wild grass
- 3–5 x allium
- 6 x Russian sage
- 1 x honesty
- 5 x pink poker statice
- 3 x jack-in-the hedge

Middle flowers

- 5 x globe thistle
- 5 x poppy
- 15 x larkspur, pastel
- 3 x feverfew
- 5 x annual statice, pale yellow
- 5 x field pennycress
- 2 x German statice
- 5 x annual statice, white
- 5 x pennycress

Show flowers

- 50 x strawflower head, pastel

Sparkle flowers

- 10 x immortelle, purple
- 5 x billy button
- 20 x paper daisy, pink
- 7 x bracken

Method

MAKE THE FRAME

1 Place your branches somewhere with space to work, like a large table or on the floor.

2 The aim is to position the branches in such a way as to form a frame with a central window. Place the branches so that they curve away from each other in the middle and cross over at both ends. It can take a bit of playing around to achieve the desired effect; there are no rules, use what you need. Spend time getting the shape right as it is a major part of the final look. My frame window is approximately 45 x 30cm (18 x 12in) in an organic lozenge shape. Don't worry about the exact size of your window; so long as it's big enough to create a small flower panel, that's all that matters. Work with the natural flow of the materials you have.

3 Once you are happy with the shape and size of your branch frame, wrap binding wire around the sections where the branches cross over each other to hold them together and to create a firm structure.

4 Attach a loop of binding wire at the back of the frame and hang it on a wall. Now stand back and have a look at the overall outline. Play with the tilt, adjusting it until you like the appearance of it. This is also a good moment to trim off any unwanted twigs with secateurs or, conversely, add a few more with binding wire to achieve a better shape.

5 To create the central wire panel, roll out a length of chicken wire and place the branch frame on top of it. Using the wire cutters, cut all the way around your branch window about 4–5cm (2in) away from the outside edge; this leaves a little excess wire to mould around the sides of the frame afterwards. You can use gloves to protect your hands if you like.

6 Now take the panel of wire and place it on top of the branch window, bending the wire down around the outside branches to help hold it in place. You may need to make small slits in the wire to accommodate any side branches, if you have any. Use binding wire to 'stitch' the chicken-wire panel to the branch frame by winding it around the branch and through every other chicken-wire hole, all the way around the outside.

7 Hang the frame back on the wall, ready to decorate. Then lay out the flowers you are going to use on a nearby surface so that they are easy to get to.

DECORATE THE BASE LAYER

8 Start decorating with the longest stems, such as the grasses, allium and Russian sage. Hold them up to the twiggy frame and see where you would like them to go and what length you need. I have placed mine so that they protrude beyond the 'window' of the branch frame. Aim for a pleasing shape, where the textures complement the twig structure.

9 Once you have decided where to put a stem, thread it into the central chicken-wire mesh and weave it in and out of the holes three or four times until it has gripped firmly (see pages 40-41). Use bullion wire to tie in any stems that need extra support or positioning (see pages 40-41).

10 Keep standing back to look at the shape and outline of the design, playing with different positions until you are happy. Be bold! Tie thin stems together in small bunches with bullion wire to create clumps if it helps. Bullion wire is your friend, use it to tie in anywhere.

DECORATE THE MIDDLE LAYER

11 Now that you have an outline to your work of art, start adding some colour and body towards the centre. As above, first hold your stems up to see where you want them to go and then thread them into the chicken-wire panel until they are fixed firmly in place. It's great to play with angles at this stage and you may wish to try and achieve a slightly asymmetric feel to the design.

12 Add shorter sprigs of field pennycress and white statice to soften the edges of the frame and cover the stem bases in the chicken-wire panel; they will also provide a background for the strawflowers to nestle into.

DECORATE THE SHOW LAYER

13 Next, we create the wow factor at the heart of the sculpture, which is jam-packed with delicious strawflowers in every pastel shade, and from which everything else radiates. Add bullion wire to the strawflowers to attach them to the sculpture (see page 39).

14 Thread each wired flower through the chicken wire, tying or twisting the bullion wire at the back to keep it in place. This can be a little fiddly as there are so many other stems in the way, but there's normally a small gap to be found. Overlap the flowers slightly to cover the wire and be sure to go right to the edge of the frame and fill in all the gaps. There will be a lot of flowers in a small area, but it's worth the effort as it will look stunning!

DECORATE THE STAR LAYER

15 Now that the structure, colour and shape are in place, it's time for another appraisal to see if there are any gaps or missing elements. You may wish to add an extra strand of grass or some more strawflowers.

16 Add the last little twinkles of colour and detail, such as the immortelle, billy buttons and paper daisies.

17 Last of all, tuck a few bracken in around the edges of the central panel to enhance the outline, giving it a little burst of delicate detail here and there. It should now be a beautiful piece of floral art.

TIPS

- Substitute some of the flowers in this project for your own foraged or dried materials to make it your own.
- Keep on the lookout for interesting branches when you're out and about; they can pop up when you are least expecting it! I love collecting beautiful, sculptural wood so I have plenty of material for making things. Driftwood also works very well.
- Be adventurous with the size and shape. Don't be afraid to try your own style and design, and go with the flow of the natural, individual materials you have found. That's the beauty of it!

Prairie Flower Cloud

This project is a floating cloud of fluffy grasses and delicate flowers that captures the feeling of prairie meadows and warm summer breezes. It's wonderful to see how it reveals a changing flowerscape on every side as it gently spins. This grass sculpture is all about catching the light and bringing a soft, subtle texture into your home that is sophisticated, captivating and calming. Its sure to attract gazes of admiration and enjoyment wherever it is placed.

Perfect for

- Above tables
- Hallways
- Windows
- Stairwells
- Events or parties
- Shop or café décor
- Under pitched or high ceilings
- Above counters or desks
- Over sideboards
- Beneath rooflights
- As the centre of arches or entrances

Tools & equipment

- Wire cutters
- 3 x chicken wire, 13mm (½in) gauge holes, 30cm x 30cm (12 x 12in)
- Gloves (optional)
- Binding wire
- Floristry scissors/ secateurs
- Stick or rod, approximately 80cm (32in) long (optional)

Flowers & boughs

- 1 x large handful of moss
- 5–6 x bunches of fibreoptic grass
- 1 x bunch calamagrostis grass
- 1 x bunch squirrel tail grass
- 2 x bunches bunny tail grass
- 3 x bunches wild foraged grass
- 25–30 x strawflower, pale yellow
- 100 x paper daisy, pink
- 1–3 x pink poker statice
- 15 x bistort, pink

Method

MAKE THE WIRE CENTRE

1 Cut out three 30 x 30cm (12 x 12in) squares of chicken wire.

2 Create the wire centre by placing a large handful of moss in the centre of one of the pieces of chicken wire and carefully scrunching the edges around it to form a small 10cm (4in) ball. Take care of sharp wire ends and wear gloves if you need to. Tuck the sharp wire ends into the centre of the ball.

3 Place this ball in the middle of the second square of chicken wire and gently scrunch the wire around it, so that there is a slight gap between it and the previous layer.

4 Repeat this process with the third square of chicken wire to create a nice, round ball shape that is approximately 15cm (6in) in diameter. You should now have three chicken-wire balls sitting inside each other, meaning there will be plenty of holes to insert your stems into from any angle.

5 Once you are happy with the shape and size of the ball, wrap binding wire around it several times from every angle to secure the layers and hold it together nice and firmly.

6 Attach a 15cm (6in) loop of binding wire to the top of the ball and suspend it at roughly shoulder height, so that you can comfortably decorate both the top and underside of the cloud.

DECORATE THE FLOWER CLOUD

7 To start with, cover the entire wire ball with a layer of fibreoptic grass. I have done this in two ways. One is by making small bunches of grass, containing around ten stems, wired together at the base to create a pointed tip for poking into the centre of the wire ball (see step 8). The other is by pushing individual grass stems into the ball. A mixture of both ensures an even covering that is not too time consuming.

8 To make the small bunches of grass, pre-cut a handful of 10cm (4in) binding wire lengths and then cut ten or so grass stems to approximately 20–25cm (8–10in) long. Pick up a piece of your binding wire and wrap it firmly in a spiral down the last 5cm (2in) of the stems to form a point at the end. Face any wire ends upwards so they don't catch as you push the bunch into the wire ball. Insert the bunch into the moss then gently separate the stems slightly to fluff them out.

9 As the wire ball fills up, you may find it helpful to push a stick or rod horizontally through the centre of the wire ball to act as a temporary handle to hold onto as you work. This helps to hold the cloud steady while pushing flowers into it and to turn it.

10 Once the fibreoptic grass layer has been completed, start to create some structure and design. Place the calamagrostis grass, squirrel tail grass, bunny tail grass and wild grasses in asymmetric clusters around the cloud. Stand back and spin the ball to check how it looks from every angle. This may take a little bit of trial and error, so have a play with it and try different positions out. For the bunny tail grass, it may be easier to put them into small bunches, as you did for the fibreoptic grass, using the wire technique in step 8.

11 Now your cloud design has some structure you can add some drifts of colour with the yellow strawflowers and pink paper daisies. I recommend wiring together small bunches of paper daisies (see step 8) as their stems can be very delicate and are liable to break. The strawflowers can be pushed in individually. I have threaded both carefully through the grasses in drifts to achieve impact. I have kept my colours in succinct, separate areas to achieve a stronger effect, but you can blend them together if you like. Again, check the cloud from every angle as you work and make any adjustments.

12 For a final flourish, place a long, wiggly pink poker statice or two at the top of the cloud and a cluster of fluffy pink bistort underneath for an extra little flash of colour and texture to bring it alive. Remove the stick handle, spin your ball and enjoy!

TIPS

- Substitute fibreoptic grass for field pennycress or lady's mantle as an alternative covering texture.
- Reduce or increase the number of flowers for a more minimal or more colourful effect.
- This is a great project for using fresh wild grasses that can dry in situ. Forage different textured and coloured grasses to make your own wild creation.

Vignette Tablescape

Perfect for

- Tables
- Weddings
- Windows
- Parties and events
- Sideboards
- Mantels and shelves

Tools & equipment

- 4 x small pin frogs, 3.5–5cm (1½–2in)
- 4 x small bowls, the ones used here are 5cm (2in) wide at the base, 12cm (4¾in) wide at the top and 5.5cm (2¼in) high
- 8 x small vases and bottles, ranging from 5–15cm (2–6in) high
- Floristry scissors/ secateurs

Flowers & boughs

- 10 x dahlia, pink
- 14 x ranunculus, pastel
- 7 x globe thistle
- 1 x poppy
- 1 x billy button
- 9 x larkspur, grey
- 5 x German statice
- 3 x fern
- 5 x gypsophilia
- 3 x paper daisy, pink
- 12 x strawflower, pale pink

This collection of flowers evokes pure and simple elegance. I like to think of it as a ballet performance of pirouetting flowers working together to produce a stunning show. The aim of this display is to ensure that each individual flower is appreciated for its simple beauty, while at the same time complementing its neighbour and creating a beautiful collective effect. If possible, I find it best to create this project in situ, so that you can see exactly how it will look as you put it together.

Method

1 Place the pin frogs into the centre of each bowl.

2 Arrange the bowls, vases, bottles and flowers on the table so you can easily reach them.

3 Starting with the bowls, we will be using seven or eight stems per bowl, choosing from the dahlia, ranunculus, globe thistle, poppy and billy button. You can either use a single variety in each bowl or group them together; here I have a mixture of single variety bowls and combinations. To make each bowl, either push the stems carefully onto the pins so they push up into the centre of the stems, or wedge the stems between the pins to hold them firmly in place. Turn the bowl as you work and arrange the flowers in varying heights of approximately 15–50cm (6–20in) so they splay outwards from the centre and look good from every angle.

4 Next, choose four of the tallest vases or bottles and place three stems of larkspur in three of them, then three stems of ranunculi in the other. Once again, slightly vary the heights and stem angles so that they complement each other.

5 In the smaller vases, create four arrangements varying in size using the German statice, fern, gypsophilia, paper daisies and strawflowers. These will act as the lower tier of the collection.

6 Try out different positions for your bowls and vases until you feel it is perfectly harmonious and balanced.

TIPS

- Arrange the bowls and vases so the tallest are in the centre and the smallest are at the edges.
- Take time to explore how the flowers sit in relation to each other, looking for different stem lengths, shapes and bends to enhance the delicate contrast.
- As an alternative to pin frogs, make your own stem holders from modelling clay.

3

NEUTRALS

White Meadow Lampshade

Making your own flower meadow lampshade is a treat for the senses and adds a unique look to any room. The chicken wire allows maximum light to filter through, illuminating the stunning textures and natural colours. It looks beautiful in daylight, as well as at night with the light turned on, throwing atmospheric shadows around the room. I have made a 30 x 25cm (12 x 10in) table lampshade.

Perfect for

- Bedrooms
- Office spaces
- Sitting rooms or lounges
- Kitchens
- Side tables or sideboards
- Mantels
- Shelves

Tools & equipment

- Chicken wire, 13mm (½in) mesh holes, 98 x 27cm (38 x 10½in)
- 2 x wire lamp rings, 30cm (12in) diameter
- Gloves (optional)
- Wire cutters
- Binding wire
- Floristry scissors/secateurs
- Bullion wire

Flowers & boughs

Base flowers

- 7 x larkspur, white
- 20 x wild grasses

Filler flowers

- 7 x rudbeckia seed head
- 5 x sea holly
- 6 x aquilegia seed head
- 5 x canary grass
- 10 x lesser quaking grass
- 10 x bunny tail grass
- 5 x honesty
- 5 x bladder campion
- 6 x field pennycress
- 7 x *Achillea ptarmica* 'The Pearl'

Show flowers

- 10 x globe thistle
- 15–20 x strawflower, white
- 5 x dahlia, white
- 6 x velvet leaf
- 10 x winged everlasting
- 5 x annual statice, white
- 15 x immortelle, white
- 15 x paper daisy, white

Method

MAKE THE LAMPSHADE

1 Unroll a section of chicken wire and place the spoked wire lamp ring on its side along the outer edge of the wire. Take care of sharp edges and use gloves if you wish. Working with the natural curl of the chicken wire, wrap it all the way around the lamp ring until it overlaps slightly by 2–3cm (¾–1in) to allow for wiring together.

2 Using the wire cutters, cut along this line, away from the outer edge, to a depth of 27cm (10½in) and then, from there, cut a line paralell to the lamp-ring edge, creating a rectangular panel of chicken wire approximately 98cm (38in) x 27cm (10½in)

3 Cut a 1m (40in) length of binding wire and attach it to a corner of your chicken wire panel. Place your spoked lamp ring along the longest edge making sure the dish for the lightbulb fitting is facing inwards. Start to stitch the edge of the chicken wire onto the lamp ring by threading the binding wire through the mesh holes and around the ring. I stitch through every other hole and find this is strong enough.

4 Once you have stitched all the way around the first ring, repeat this process with the other ring. With both rings attached to the chicken wire, you should have a drum shape approximately 25cm (10in) high.

5 Using another length of wire, stitch down the side seam to complete the shade.

ADD THE DECORATION

6 Before you start to decorate your shade, decide whether it will be for a table lamp (as here) or a ceiling light. If it is for a table lamp, make sure the spoked metal lampshade ring with the lightbulb fitting is at the *bottom*; if it is for a ceiling light, make sure it is at the *top*.

As you decorate, consider where the lightbulb will be visible from inside the shade when it's switched on. Apply a few more flowers at this level to help better obscure it from view.

Take a moment to think about your design and to prepare your flowers into handy piles to work from. I have chosen predominantly textures and fillers rather than flowers to achieve a delicate, slightly see-through, natural look, but this balance can be totally to your taste.

7 To start, choose some tall, stemmed flowers, such as larkspur, and thread them in place at regular intervals around the drum to divide the design into quarters or fifths (see pages 40–41). This breaks the area down into easily manageable sections to fill in and helps to achieve an even design that looks good from all angles.

8 Apply the other longer stems, such as grasses, as the base layer. Consider how much you would like some of these stems to reach above the top of the shade. I think it looks lovely have a few pretty grasses wiggling up and catching the light.

9 Now start to place the other flowers and fillers lower down. This is all the remaining flowers, either applied in drifts of the same thing or evenly spaced throughout the design. For some of the flowers I like to place a few stems close together, creating more impact. Spin the shade around as you work and check for an even distribution of flowers. The strawflowers, globe thistles and dahlias are the most prominent focal points, so make sure these stand out in key locations throughout the design.

10 Use silver bullion wire to add support and extra strength to the strawflowers and paper daisies (see page 40). Wire stemless flower heads and short stems directly onto the chicken wire (see page 39).

11 Once you are happy with a good, even distribution of flowers and your lampshade is looking beautiful from every angle, pop it on a lamp base to check how it looks with the light switched on. This is a great moment to add the odd strategic flower to help obscure the bulb or a few more strands to stick above the shade to catch the light.

TIPS

- If you don't have a huge selection of flowers to choose from, try a simple palette of a couple of different white flower varieties repeated around the lampshade. A simple design can be very effective.
- Adjust the depth of your lampshade by increasing or decreasing the height of the wire when you make it to create different looks.

Circular Flower Panel

A round flower panel offers a lovely shape that really stands out. It allows you to play with the flower design within its frame, creating a superb focal point that will lift any room. As I put together this design, I had in mind a woodland glade, dappled in shade, with ferns and grasses among a carpet of dazzling white flowers catching the sunbeams. This colour palette may be cool and sophisticated, but it is also dancing with life and energy, and is a splendid way to enjoy everlasting flowers.

Perfect for

- Windows
- Walls
- Weddings
- Shelves or mantels
- Bedrooms
- Screens
- Above fireplaces
- Hallways, landings or stairways

Tools & equipment

- Cardboard, 55 x 55cm (21½ x 21½in)
- String
- Tape measure
- Large pin or sharp pencil
- Pen or pencil
- Scissors
- Binding wire
- Chicken wire, 13mm (½in) gauge holes, 57 x 57cm (22½ x 22½in)
- Gloves (optional)
- Wire cutters
- Floristry scissors/ secateurs
- Bullion wire

Flowers & boughs

Base flowers

- 3 x willow rod, 5–7mm (¼in) thick
- 25 x wild foraged grass
- 5 x Chinese silver grass
- 5 x foxtail millet grass
- 10 x royal fern

Filler flowers

- 5 x larkspur, white
- 8 x annual statice, white
- 10 x aquilegia seed head
- 7 x achillea, white

Show flowers

- 5 x dahlia, white
- 15 x strawflower, white
- 35 x paper daisy, white
- 10 x cornflower, white

Sparkle flowers

- 5 x billy button
- 1 x bunch bunny tail grass
- 5 x shepherd's purse

Method

MAKE THE TEMPLATE

1 Start by placing a sheet of cardboard on a flat work surface. Create a rudimentary compass using a length of string with a loop tied at each end. The total length of the string, including these loops, should be roughly half the width of the intended circle; my circle is 55cm (22in) across, so my string was 27.5cm (11in) long.

2 Put a pin or sharp pencil through one of the loops in the string and firmly position it in the centre of the cardboard sheet. With the other hand, place a pen or pencil through the second loop while pulling the string taut. Keeping a tight hold on both points, slowly draw the outline of a circle by moving the pen or pencil around the central pin.

3 Cut out the circle template with scissors.

MAKE THE FRAME

4 Select three willow rods. They will need a bit of 'flexing' to take on a nice curve but so they don't snap when bending. To do this, hold a rod with two hands and gently but firmly press outwards, using both of your thumbs, every 3–4cm (2–3in) or so along their length to gently encourage the willow to stretch into shape and become more pliable. Repeat with the other rods. Don't worry if you break one or two, sometimes it takes a couple of goes to get it right.

5 Bend each rod around to follow the circle template, overlapping each one a third of the way along its length and winding binding wire around them to hold them together. Once you have all three willow rods wired together in this way, curve them around to complete the circle, using the template as a guide; adjust if necessary, before wiring the circle together.

6 Shape your frame into a satisfactory circle by pushing the willow out with your thumbs for any final adjustments.

7 Unroll a section of chicken wire and fold it back slightly to flatten it out (weigh down the corners with something heavy if it helps). Wire can be very springy and unpredictable, with sharp edges, so take care and wear gloves if you need to.

8 Place your cardboard template over the wire and, using wire cutters, create a circle following the template but approximately 1–2cm (½–¾in) away from the edge. This will allow extra for folding in the sharp wire ends afterwards.

9 Once you have cut all the way around, and while your template is still in place, carefully fold the sharp edges of your chicken wire no more than two-thirds of the way inwards, over the cardboard, to crease your panel edges. This way you will still be able to remove the template afterwards.

10 Remove the cardboard from the centre and flatten the wire edges the rest of the way down. Check your wire panel is the correct size by placing the template underneath it. Make any minor adjustments to size at this stage by manipulating the wire, if needed.

11 Cut a 1m (3ft) or an arm's length of binding wire and attach it to the willow frame. Place the frame around your wire circle and 'stitch' it to the edge of the mesh using binding wire. Do this by wrapping the wire around the willow and through the honeycomb holes along the wire-mesh edge. Keep a firm tension, sewing through every second hole and pulling the wire tight as you go until you have sewn all the way around.

12 Check the frame against the template afterwards and pull into a final, satisfactory shape.

13 Tie a length of binding wire at the top of your circle to hang it from.

ADD THE BASE LAYER

14 Working either on a wall or at a table, thread the longest wild grasses down through the chicken wire to fix them in place (see pages 40–41). I have arranged them so that some of the stems stick up above the frame, which helps to give a sense of movement to the design.

15 Think about the shape and layout of the design, and ask yourself how much of the space you want to fill. Leaving a small area at the top of the design empty allows the outline of the grasses to be appreciated and helps to keep it looking delicate. You could curve the design to follow the frame shape slightly, with a few escaping fronds; it's up to you.

16 Place different grass textures in clumps to create a stronger impact; the Chinese silver grass and foxtail millet are both great for this.

17 Wire the ferns directly onto the chicken wire at the base of the design using a small length of bullion wire at the top and bottom of each leaf and fastening at the back (see page 41).

ADD THE FILLER LAYER

18 Continue adding flowers in the same way as the grasses. Use the larkspur, statice, aquilegia and achillea to fill space and build texture, layering them over the grass stems in beautiful flowing lines.

ADD THE SHOW LAYER

19 Carefully place the dahlias as the main focal point to the design, before adding the strawflowers, paper daisies and cornflowers in between them.

ADD THE SPARKLE LAYER

20 I have added a few pops of billy buttons in the top centre of my design as I love a tiny bit of contrasting colour to set things off.

21 Place a few bunny tail grasses in sprays throughout the design and around the edges to fill any gaps and add a little white, fluffy pizzazz.

22 Lastly, weave in a few stems of shepherd's purse around the edges for a few wayward sparks.

TIPS

- To save time, use pre-made metal or wooden hoops instead of the willow frame.
- Press and dry ferns between sheets of cardboard in the summer to use all year round.
- If you don't have dried ferns to hand, any dried leaves will do; bracken or eucalyptus are great alternatives.

Statement Vase

An opulent and majestic flower display like this radiates class and sophistication. Large and dramatic, its stylish, asymmetric design gives it a modern edge. It would work equally well in a minimal setting or in a luxurious parlour. The incredible textures and muted colour palette make this a wonderfully creative but beautifully simple arrangement to make. What's not to love!

Perfect for

- Sideboards
- Weddings
- Hallways
- Mantels
- Focal points
- Tables
- Parties or events
- Shop or café décor
- Business receptions
- Kitchens

Tools & equipment

- Chicken wire, 13mm (½in) gauge holes, 30 x 30cm (12 x 12in) or more to suit vase shape and size
- Wire cutters
- Gloves (optional)
- Large pot or vase, minimum 23cm (9in) tall with a 10cm (4in) opening
- Floristry scissors/ secateurs

Flowers & boughs

- 3 x German statice
- 6 x pearly everlasting
- 5 x pennycress
- 1 x honesty, purple, 80cm (35in)
- 3 x Persian cress
- 5 x bladder wrack
- 25 x bunny tail grass
- 1 x hydrangea, green
- 3 x love-lies-bleeding
- 4 x foxtail millet grass
- 3 x camassia, white/ green, 90cm (35in) tall
- 2 x common reed grass, light, 1m (40in)
- 8–10 x ranunculus, white
- 2 x dahlia, white
- 7 x billy button
- 5 x common reed grass, black
- 1–2 x poppy seed head
- 2 x pink poker statice
- 1 x contorted hazel, 1m (40in)
- 3 x wild feathery grass, 1m (40in)

Method

CREATE A STEM SUPPORT

1 Cut out a 30cm (12in) square piece of chicken wire with the wire cutters or use an offcut. (Make this a little bigger or smaller as necessary to suit the size of your pot.)

2 Scrunch the chicken wire into a cylinder shape that will fit snuggly into the bottom two-thirds of the pot without damaging it as it goes in. Use gloves to protect your hands if you like. Carefully push the wire cylinder down into your pot until it is firmly in place, ready for you to start work.

ADD THE FLOWERS

3 Add short flowers to form a base and provide extra support for other stems. Position the German statice to fill the centre, followed by the pearly everlasting on one side and the pennycress on the other. Push the stems down through the chicken wire into the pot so they all sit securely. I love to place the flowers in gentle clumps to help achieve definition and drama.

4 Now that you have a nice base, it's time to add the central structure. This is where it's important to work on finding the asymmetric style and shape of the design. Position the large purple honesty stem at the back to one side and then a cluster of Persian cress on the opposite side, followed by the bladder wrack and bunny tail grass in between. Then tuck the hydrangea in at the front. Stand back to check you're happy with how it's looking.

5 Next, add some drama and shape with the back and side structure. Place the love-lies-bleeding and the foxtail millet on one side, the tall, statuesque camassia at the back, followed by the light common reed grass on the opposite side. It may take a few attempts to find the right position for these, so be prepared to have a play until you're happy with it.

6 With the main structure in place, you can position the stars of the show. Place a drift of white ranunculi at the front so they can really be appreciated. The dahlias can be tucked in below to help cover the stem bases. Next, place a spray of billy buttons to the side, then use the black common reed grass to fill in between. Insert the poppy seed heads next to the billy buttons and pop in one or two pink poker statice to help add balance and movement where needed.

7 Lastly, after standing back to check you are happy, place the contorted hazel and the tall wild grass stems to provide the last bit of shimmer and balance to complete the look. Voila, you're done!

TIPS

- Finding the best flower positions to achieve this relaxed, asymmetric design can take a bit of refining and practice, so it's okay to move things around until you feel you've achieved the right balance. Allow yourself the time and space to enjoy the process.
- The lighting and background can make a huge difference to how a display like this can look. Try it out in different locations to find the most beautiful effect.

Winter Mantel

For a surprisingly simple set of ingredients and steps, this mantel display is fantastically grand. The effect it had on this room was a total revelation. The space was lovely to start with, but these twigs and flowers brought a wild, otherworldly quality to it that turned it into an extra special, luxurious place to be. The materials, flowers and mechanics used to create the display help ensure it is robust enough to cope with the heat of the fire, and the pale colours used throughout mean it does not fade too much.

Perfect for

- Mantels and fire surrounds
- Shelves
- Around doorways and windows
- Sideboards
- Winter and Christmas décor

Tools & equipment

- Floristry scissors
- Binding wire
- Secateurs

Flowers & boughs

Show flowers

- 30 x strawflower, white
- 150 x winged everlasting

Base flowers

- 2 x large hazel boughs, to fit the side and top of your fire surround; these were 130cm (51in) and 120cm (47in) long
- 2–3 x medium hazel branch, 50–70cm (20–28in) long

Filler flowers

- 3–4 x traveller's joy, 1–2m (40–80in) long
- 15 x honesty, 20–30cm (8–10in) long
- 15 x velvet leaf

Method

PREPARE THE FLOWERS

1 First, prepare the strawflowers by trimming with floristry scissors and wiring the flower heads to create wire stems so they can be attached to the branches later (see page 39).

2 Prepare 20 small bunches of winged everlasting ready to be placed among the branches later. To make these, select five to eight stems of winged everlasting, then wind a 15cm (6in) length of binding wire around the last 10cm (4in) of the stem ends.

MAKE THE BRANCH SURROUND

3 Position one of the two larger hazel branches along the top of your mantel and the other up the side. It's worth taking a bit of time adjusting the branches until they sit nicely together as these are the foundations and outline of your design. I've used a slimmer branch for the side and a fuller one for the top to create an asymmetric sweep up to the far end. Stand back to check you're happy with the overall appearance, then trim off any unwanted twigs with secateurs to achieve a nice shape. Use binding wire to attach the side branch and top branch together where they meet at the corner, and to position any other twigs that may need pulling in.

4 Use the medium hazel branches to blend the join between the side and the top branches and to fill in any gaps along the top; wire them in place with binding wire if necessary. Stand back and check the design from a distance to ensure it is balanced and looking good.

ADD THE FILLER FLOWERS

5 Once you are happy with the background, gently tease the stems of traveller's joy along the top of the display, tucking them into the branches slightly and wiring them in place if necessary. Leave a couple of tendrils to trail over the corners and down the sides slightly at each end to create a delicate, wispy feel.

6 Next, place the beautiful, light-catching stems of honesty among the branches of the main body of the display, wiring them to the branches if they need it.

7 Use the velvet leaf stems to help enhance the shape and movement of the design by carefully placing them to complement the outline of the branches. Once again, stand back to check the overall look. Wire them to the branches and other stems to hold them in position, and use a few stems to trail over the front edge of the mantel and tumble over the ends.

ADD THE SHOW FLOWERS

8 Now the framework is complete, it's time to add the flowers you prepared earlier. Position the 20 bunches of winged everlasting throughout the design, teasing out the bunches slightly to create a delicate haze of white that can be appreciated throughout. Use a few bunches to spray over the front and sides of the mantel.

9 Lastly, as the display is nearing completion, make it really shine by attaching the pre-wired strawflower heads directly onto the branches and other stems. You can create a beautiful cluster at either end of the display, so that you can clearly appreciate their impact from a distance.

TIPS

- Use pot tape or drawing pins and wire to attach the hazel twigs to the mantel if you need a bit of extra support to hold the display in place.
- Any nice-looking branches will work in place of hazel – use whatever is available to you. Birch and beech branches are great alternatives.
- Depending on the orientation of the fireplace in your room, you can swap which side the branches go up by reversing the design.

Wild & White Ceiling Decoration

This suspended ceiling decoration is surprisingly simple to create considering the impact it makes to a space. It is dramatic yet delicate, catching the light and casting soft shadows. It has real presence and brings an understated glamour to its surroundings. I love the creative freedom of expression I feel when making something wild and ethereal like this. Please note, this project will require a fixing from above to hang your creation while you work.

Perfect for

- Above tables
- Hallways
- Above entrances
- Weddings
- Ceiling spaces
- Yurt or marquee canopies
- Stairwells
- Window displays

Tools & equipment

- Wire cable with clip to hang the decoration from (optional)
- Binding wire
- Secateurs/floristry scissors
- Bullion wire

Flowers & boughs

Frame

- 50–100 x willow rod, 5–10mm (⅛–⅜in) thick

Base flowers

- 10 x small corkscrew hazel branch, or similar characterful branches
- 11 x birch branch

Show flowers

- 25 x German statice
- 25 x honesty
- 25 x Persian cress

Sparkle flowers

- 50 x strawflower bud, white
- 50 x astrantia head, white

Method

MAKE THE FRAME

1 Start by making a 60cm (2ft) willow ring, which will be the base for the decoration (see pages 42–43).

HANG THE WILLOW RING

2 Attach a length of wire from the ceiling; this will be the central hanging point for your decoration and will allow you to spin it easily as you work. If you have a cable with a clip at each end this can help but, otherwise, double strands of binding wire will do. Make it long enough to work at a comfortable height.

3 Cut three 1m (3ft) lengths of binding wire, wrap them around the willow ring and secure them in three evenly spaced places around the circle. Take the three wire strands together to a central point, then tie them to your ceiling-mounted central wire, adjusting the lengths so that the willow ring is horizontally level and approximately head height. Tie firmly to secure in place.

ADD THE TWIGGY BASE LAYER

4 Take your corkscrew hazel (or alternatives). Cut them into manageable sized branches with secatuers before fixing them to the outside of the willow ring. Attach them securely in place by wrapping binding wire around both the hazel branches and the willow ring, taking care to keep it looking nice and relaxed with plenty of movement. Hold each branch up as you work to see how it looks.

5 As you lay the hazel branches around the ring, make sure to have some of the twigs sticking up above the ring as well as down below and out sideways. I have made mine quite wild, with the branches extending anything from 20–40cm (8–16in) in all directions. This increases the overall size of the decoration to around 1m (3ft) wide and 80cm (2½ft) deep, but you can adjust this to suit the final location. Intertwine the butt-ends of the branches into each other where possible, tying them in place using binding wire.

6 This is the main structure and outline for the piece, so take time to create a beautiful overall shape at this stage. Spin the ring as you work to make sure it looks good from every angle, filling in any gaps. Once you are happy with the first structural layer, go around the ring with a reel of binding wire to make sure it's all firmly held together.

7 Apply a few birch twigs. Take a selection of varying lengths of birch, from 20–40cm (8–16in), then cut the stems at an angle to create a sharp point to help with sliding them into place.

8 To attach the birch twigs, push the pointed ends carefully under the wire wound around the willow ring, poking the ends in between the willow rods underneath, until you can feel that it is gripping firmly in place. Position the birch in between the hazel branches to help hide any branch ends and fill any gaps. Add a few around the inside edge of the willow ring so that it looks good from below.

ADD THE FLOWERS

9 Using the same attachment method as the birch, insert sprigs of German statice evenly around the ring in between the twigs on the sides, top and bottom. This will help to camouflage the willow ring.

10 Prepare your honesty by stripping away any seed sheaths so they are bright and shimmering white. The honesty branches can range from 20–40cm (8–16in) in length and are used to create an illuminating asymmetric outline. Insert in the same way as the birch and statice. I have tucked a few small pieces in all the way around, but have then mainly focussed on two or three areas where I have placed more for extra impact; they spray out in all directions to create a sense of drama. Spin the decoration around to view this effect from every angle.

11 Insert a few delicate stems of Persian cress to add a little sparkly texture. These can vary in length and be placed anywhere that needs a little filling in.

12 To complete the look, create a few flower tendrils to delicately trail from the branches below. Ranging in length from 30cm (12in) to 60cm (2ft) I have made fourteen strands in total: seven with strawflower buds and seven with astrantia flowers. You can use any small white flower as an alternative.

Make the flower strands by choosing flower heads with a short 1–2cm (½–1in) stem to attach the wire to. It helps to have the flowers prepared beforehand. Select a length of silver bullion wire and carefully but firmly wrap the wire around the stem of a flower, with the head facing downwards. Repeat this process every 5–10cm (2–4in) along the length of wire. I have attached my flowers with the largest flower at the top of the wire, decreasing in size to the smallest at the bottom.

13 Once you have decorated all fourteen wires, tie the strands to the twigs on the underside of the ring at varying intervals, creating gorgeous, ethereal flower vines to catch the light.

TIPS

- If it's not easy to fix a hanging wire from a ceiling to work from, try using a free-standing metal clothes rail instead. This is also a great way of transporting your decoration if necessary.
- You can use foraged ivy branches as a substitute for the corkscrew hazel.
- As an alternative to the willow ring, you could use a pre-made metal or wooden ring and wrap it with chicken wire.

Everlasting Blossom Tree

There are times when you want to make an impact in a large space, and this must be one of the most simple, elegant and effective ways of achieving that using everlasting flowers. I get so excited by the possibilities of scale with these blossom trees. Their airy and delicate structures catch the light beautifully, complementing many different locations and situations. They also look glorious en masse.

Perfect for

- Weddings
- Marqueess or tents
- Festivals, parties or events
- Entranceways
- Windows
- Anywhere in the home
- Show stands
- Shop, café or restaurant décor

Tools & equipment

- Drill
- Flat drill-bit to match the diameter of the branch base
- Sharp knife (optional)
- Bullion wire
- Floristry scissors/ secateurs
- Binding wire

Flowers & boughs

- 1 x large hazel branch or equivalent; I have used a 2m (6ft 6in) branch
- 1 x log, 20–30 x 20–30cm (6–12 x 6–12in), for the stand (optional)
- 75 x strawflower head, white
- 5–10 x honesty
- 5–10 x German statice
- 10 x hydrangea head, green

Method

PREPARE THE BASE AND TREE

1 Find a large, beautifully proportioned hazel branch or equivalent. The one I have used is approximately 2m (6ft 6in) high, which will easily fit in most rooms. When selecting a branch, choose one that has an attractive overall shape and is well balanced, so that it looks good from every angle. Check how straight the stem is; this can affect how upright it will sit. A crooked stem may look characterful, but it can be slightly more challenging to get it to sit nicely in a log base or vase.

2 Create a base for your branch to sit in by selecting a round log or a square-cut chunk of wood. The log must have a flat top and bottom, and needs to be heavy and large enough to support the branch above it. If you are using a lighter-weight wood, like pine, you may need a larger log to gain enough base weight.

3 Before you drill a hole in the centre of the log, carefully look at the shape of branch stem. If it isn't perfectly straight, you may want to drill your hole at a slight angle to get the desired upright position.

4 Drill a hole using a flat drill bit to a depth of roughly 3–5cm (1–2in). Push the branch down into the hole, making sure it's a good, snug fit. If it's too tight, shave slivers off the end of the branch with a sharp knife; if it's a little loose, tap small chunks of wood in around the edges to firm it up.

PREPARE THE FLOWERS

5 Prepare the strawflower heads by threading them with a single piece of binding wire (see page 39).

6 Remove the papery outer seed shells from the honesty to reveal the silvery inner discs, before dividing the stems into smaller pieces ready to wire directly onto the branches.

7 Similarly, cut the German statice into small sprigs ready for wiring.

8 Divide the hydrangea heads into smaller sections (roughly three to five pieces from each hydrangea head). Fix stem wires onto each one ready to attach them to the branches (see page 39).

9 Cut a handful of 10cm (4in) lengths of binding wire, ready to attach the honesty and statice.

DECORATE THE TREE

10 Start with the honesty and hydrangea, as they are the bushiest elements and may obscure the smaller flowers later. Simply wire them directly onto the branches (see page 39), remembering to turn the tree as you work to make sure they are evenly distributed and facing in varied directions. Take time to check how each flower is sitting, looking for an elegant, pleasing flow to the arrangement of stems.

11 Next, wire on the statice and strawflowers in the same fashion. Disperse them generously among the honesty and hydrangea. Use some of the smaller buds and sprigs for the twig tips to add a touch of delicacy.

12 Take a few moments to stand back and survey how it's looking. Check for any bare patches or gaps that need filling.

TIPS

- You could use a large, heavy vase as a stand, instead of a log.
- Add a strand of fairy lights throughout the branches to make it stunningly sparkly and illuminated.
- Choose different flowers and colours, depending on what's available to you. That's the beauty of this design, you only need a tree branch and a box of flower heads for amazing results!
- Scale this blossom tree design up or down to suit individual situations. The sky's the limit with size, just adjust flower numbers accordingly.

Branch & Flower Frame

Most of the materials for this natural and wild design can be foraged from a hedgerow. It makes me think of woodland realms where magic takes place. The focus is on using materials and flowers with interesting colours, textures and personalities, combining to make something subtly exquisite where the detail can really be admired. I have used this frame to bring alive an old mirror, which has been transformed into a beautiful, nature-inspired focal piece.

Perfect for

- Around mirrors
- Picture surrounds
- Photo frames
- Banners
- Stand-alone frames
- Sign edging
- Name framing
- Weddings
- Parties and events
- Festivals

Tools & equipment

- Mirror or picture frame (optional)
- Secateurs/floristry scissors
- Binding wire

Flowers & boughs

- 4 x hazel branch, 80–100cm (32–40in) long, or similar branch of your choice; this is to make a 40 x 50cm (16 x 20in) frame surround
- 3 x common reed grass, dark
- 3 x foxtail millet grass, green
- 10 x wild grass
- 3 x orach, green
- 1 x poppy
- 1 x love-in-a-mist
- 2 x billy button
- 1 x velvet leaf
- 2 x honesty
- 6 x fern
- 3 x tansy
- 3 x German statice
- 1 x fennel flower
- 5 x gypsophila

Method

MAKE THE TWIG FRAME

1 Place the branches around your mirror or picture frame, taking a bit of time to play around and adjust them until you are happy with the effect. Don't worry too much if they overlap the corners a little bit as this can create a pretty detail. Trim off any branches that get in the way or you don't need with secateurs/floristry scissors, but keep most of the side branches until after you've wired the frame together.

2 Set the frame aside. Starting with the bottom corners of the branch rectangle, use a 50cm (20in) length of binding wire to wrap around each corner to secure it firmly. Stand back and check the basic shape, making sure it aligns with your picture frame.

3 Use binding wire to secure any additional branches you want to keep that cross over the corners of the frame to further strengthen the overall structure. It should feel fairly sturdy now and be possible to lift up in one piece.

4 Stand back and check how the frame is looking. Gently tie in any twigs that stick out too far with a length of binding wire to retain them if needed. Trim off any unwanted branches to finish off the shape you desire.

DECORATE WITH FLOWERS

5 Now create the main flower corner arrangement. You do this by creating a separate posy, which is then secured to the branch frame. Start with the tallest stems, which will form the background. Place the common reed grass, foxtail millet and wild grasses in your non-dominant hand and hold them against the branch frame to help gauge the size and arrange how they look. Choose how wild you would like it to appear, with stems sticking up or escaping from the sides.

6 Add texture to the mid-section of the design with the orach, poppy, love-in-a-mist, billy buttons and velvet leaf. Once again, keep holding the arrangement up every now and then to check the position of the flowers and how it looks against the branch frame.

7 Finally, fill out the bottom corner to form a fan shape. I have used honesty and ferns to establish the edges and corner, and then filled in the centre with tansy, German statice, fennel and gypsophila. Keep holding your arrangement up to the frame to check the shape and style.

8 Once you are happy with your design, tie the stems securely together with binding wire and trim the stems to size.

9 Attach the arrangement securely to the bottom corner of the frame and halfway up the side using binding wire.

10 Make any final adjustments by tucking in additional stems as needed to perfect the shape and removing any small frame twigs that may look awkward now the flowers are in place.

11 On the remaining sides of the frame, wire individual bracken fronds and gypsophila stems directly onto the branches so they delicately trail around the frame and pull the magic of the design together (see pages 38–39).

TIPS

- Adjust the size of the branches to suit any size frame.
- If you want to make a freestyle frame, draw the outline you would like on a piece of card to use as a size and shape guide instead of a picture frame.
- Take time to play around with the shape and design. This is rather like making a twig jigsaw. It can be great fun finding the best shape and contour combinations.

Magical Flower Vine

The natural, relaxed simplicity of these vines means that, not only are they easy to make, but, due to their flexible wire base, they can be twisted into any shape and placed in a multitude of locations. They capture a magical look, achieving minimalism and opulence all at the same time, with their delicate detail and wild, flowing design.

Perfect for

- Banisters
- Windows or doors
- Pillars or posts
- Archways
- Cupboard tops
- Walls
- Ceiling décor
- Parties or events
- Weddings
- Tables

Tools & equipment

- Rustic grapevine wire
- Tape measure
- Wire cutters
- Floristry scissors/ secateurs
- Binding wire

Flowers & boughs

- 30 x birch twig, 15–30cm (6–12in)
- 20 x bracken frond
- 20 x honesty
- 25–30 x German statice
- 25 x quaking grass
- 15 x gypsophilia 'Single White'
- 20–25 x field pennycress
- 20–30 x bunny tail grass
- 40 x paper daisy, white
- 40 x winged everlasting
- 25 x annual statice, white

Method

1 Prepare the birch twigs and flowers by cutting to size and positioning them for easy assembly. Stem length can be anything between 10–30cm (4–12in).

2 Measure, cut and straighten out a length of rustic grapevine wire on a work surface. This one is approximately 3m (10ft) long.

3 Tie a reel of binding wire to the end of the grapevine wire, ready to continuously bind the twigs and flowers in position along the whole length.

4 To make your vine, lay a couple stems at a time along the length of the grapevine wire with the flowers facing away from the end. Wrap the binding wire firmly around both the grapevine wire and the first quarter of each twig or flower, leaving plenty of stem to wiggle out from the vine. Layer the next stem partially over the previous one so that it faces in the same direction and hides the end slightly. Wrap in place with binding wire. Continue adding stems and wrapping them with binding wire along the length of your grapevine wire.

5 To achieve balance, place flowers on both sides of the grapevine wire, as well as to the front.

6 Create movement to the design by placing bolder stems, such as bracken or statice, on opposite sides and at staggered intervals so that they spray outwards.

7 Create depth to the design by adding a few longer stems, then covering the wire and stem ends with a few shorter ones.

8 Attach clusters of the smaller flowers and grasses at the same time so that they have more impact; groups of three to six flowers works well.

9 The distribution of flowers and textures can be random and varied so long as the vine achieves overall balance and colour. Have fun playing with how it looks and find the effect you like.

10 Once you have decorated the entire length of your grapevine wire, go back and check for areas that require filling or perhaps need more colour; tuck additional stem ends under the existing wires to help the vine come together. A few delicate grasses and an extra spot of white here and there can really make a difference.

TIPS

- Once you've twisted and placed the vine in its final position, tuck a few extra flower stems in to make it dazzle from every angle.
- Go as wild or as neat with this style as you like. Have fun and make it your own.
- Foraged grasses and flowers can look great in the design, too.

Winter Hedgerow Wreath

This rambling, textural, nest-like circle of twigs and flowers emanates the wild outdoors and brings the winter hedgerow right into your home. Its loose, informal style belies the drama it delivers with its minimal flower palette. It can be made to any size.

Perfect for

- Bedrooms
- Doors
- Hallways
- Above fireplaces
- Kitchens
- Table backdrops
- Landings or stairways

Tools & equipment

- Secateurs
- Binding wire
- Tape measure (optional)
- Bullion wire
- Floristry scissors

Flowers & boughs

- 10 x birch branch, 1m (3ft) long, or similar flexible, fine-twigged branches
- 10 x birch branch, 30–50cm (1–1½ft) long, or similar flexible, fine-twigged branches
- 3 x hop bine, 2m (6½ft) long, or similar, such as grape vine or clematis stems
- 5 x traveller's joy, 30cm (1ft) long
- 10–15 x pussy willow
- 30 x winged everlasting
- 20 x wild grass
- 20–30 x astrantia head, white
- 20–30 x strawflower bud, white
- 2–3 x honesty

Method

MAKE THE WREATH

1 Working on a flat surface, select a few birch branches (or similar) and carefully pre-bend them into a slightly curved shape, ready to wire them together into a circle.

2 Tie the end of a reel of binding wire halfway along from the cut end of the first birch branch and, at that point, lay another branch facing in the same direction over the first so that they overlap. Wind the wire around them both, allowing the wire to be loose enough not to compact the branches too tightly but secure enough to hold them in place. Allow a few side twigs to escape as you go, so that it looks nice and relaxed.

3 Working to a curve, add more branches in the same way until you have enough to achieve your desired circle circumference.

4 Curve the two ends round to overlap each other slightly and secure them together with binding wire to form a circle. I have made this wreath 80–100cm (30–40in) wide.

5 Once you are happy with the shape and size of the initial ring, add more birch branches by pushing their cut ends into the circle. Wind binding wire around them to secure, but make sure to allow a few side twigs to escape to retain the wild look as you go. Continue adding branches in this way until you are happy with the thickness and shape of your ring.

6 Attach a hoop of binding wire to your wreath to hang it from.

DECORATE THE CIRCLE

7 Hang your wreath on a wall, so that you can stand back as you work and check the overall effect from all angles.

8 Add the hop bines or other climbing plant vines that will give the wreath its rambling feel. To do this, select a nice wiggly stem and wind it around the birch ring in concentric circles, weaving it in and out slightly. Secure it in place by taking a length of binding wire and loosely tying it into the wreath here and there, making sure to keep it feeling flowing and natural. Keep adding strands around the outside, as well as inside and in front of the wreath, until you are happy with the look.

9 Add the traveller's joy in the same way as the other climbing stems.

10 Place the stems of pussy willow around the wreath by pushing them into the heart of the birch ring and securing with bullion wire if needed.

11 Take the winged everlasting flowers and push the stems into the birch wreath in gentle clusters throughout the circle. You may need to use a bit of extra bullion wire to help secure them in place if they fail to hold.

12 Similarly, place the wild grasses in clusters around the back and inside the wreath.

13 Prepare a few lengths of white flower strands for the final, delicate embellishment. To do this, first cut the stems of the astrantia and strawflowers to 1–2cm (½–1in). Next, cut a length of silver bullion wire to attach the stems to (I have used two 2.5m/8ft lengths of wire). Then, carefully wrap the bullion wire gently but firmly around the stem of each flower head several times, repeating this every 5–10cm (2–4in) as you go.

14 Once you have completed two strands, delicately drape and wind the strands around the front and sides of the wreath, overlapping in places, until you have achieved a pleasing distribution of flowers and an attractive twining effect. Use extra bullion wire to secure the strands in place.

15 Lastly, add the honesty by pushing the short stems into the wreath before wiring them into position, putting them anywhere that a touch of shimmering white is needed.

16 Now stand back one last time and check how the wreath looks from every angle. Add any final twigs or flowers.

TIPS

- For an extra flowery version, wire more flower heads directly onto the twigs around the circle.
- You could use climbing plant vines for the base as an alternative to birch branches.
- Thread copper-wire fairy lights around the ring for a delightful twinkle.
- If you omit the winged everlasting flowers, this wreath is robust enough to cope for a short time in a slightly damp environment, such as an outside porch or bathroom.

Textured Flower Bowls

These small, delightful flower bowls are packed with character. They offer a fantastic long-lasting way of decorating. Place them where something unobtrusive but beautiful is required. Focusing in on texture and tones, they complement many situations and colour schemes and draw the eye in with their exquisite detail.

Perfect for

- Dining tables
- Weddings, parties or events
- Shelves
- Sideboards
- Individual table decorations
- Windowsills
- Mantels
- Kitchen tables
- Bedrooms
- Shop, café or reception décor

Tools & equipment

- Chicken wire (small offcuts are great for this)
- Wire cutters
- 3 x small ceramic bowls, approximately 14 x 7cm (5½ x 3in)
- Pot tape
- Floristry scissors/secateurs

Flowers & boughs

- Moss
- 3 x hydrangea head, green
- 9 x German statice
- 9 x bracken frond
- 1 x bunch eucalyptus
- 1 x bunch lady's mantle
- 1 x bunch amaranth 'Green Thumb'
- 1 x bunch pearly everlasting
- 9 x poppy seed head
- 15 x cornflower, white
- 3 x globe thistle
- 9 x bladder campion
- 6 x annual statice, white
- 1 x gypsophila 'Single White'
- 6–9 x miscanthus
- 15 x canary grass
- 9 x wild grass

Method

1 Cut an approximately 25 x 25cm (10 x 10in) square of chicken wire with wire cutters. Place a handful of moss in the centre of the chicken wire and then scrunch it up to create an overlapping, layered pad. Put this pad into a bowl; it should fit snuggly inside without sticking above the rim. Secure the pad in place with a few pieces of pot tape strapped over the top of the bowl and attached to the rim. Cover the pad with a thin layer of moss to obscure the wire. Repeat for the two other bowls.

2 Start with the larger heads and filler flowers, such as the hydrangea, German statice, bracken, eucalyptus and lady's mantle to help conceal the moss, wire and bowl edges. Cut the stems to the desired height with floristry scissors or secateurs, strip any leaves from the base and gently ease the flowers into the moss and chicken wire so that they sit firmly and at a pleasing angle. This may take a couple of attempts to get right but that's okay; it's all about taking time to create a beautiful effect.

3 Work with each flower type in all three bowls at a time to help achieve a balanced effect in every vessel and keep a coherent design theme.

4 Once you have a nicely covered base, start to position the other flowers, such as the *Amaranthus hypochondriacus*, pearly everlasting, poppy seed heads, cornflowers and globe thistles to put the design structure in place. Try to add depth to the overall look by positioning the flowers in sprays and clusters at differing heights.

5 To help conceal the bowl edges, find the natural curves in the stems and flower heads and add these to the sides of the bowl to create a trailing effect. Bladder campion, annual statice and gypsophila are great for this.

6 Every now and again, step back to check you are happy with how the bowls are looking from a distance as a group and from all angles of the table. Also keep an eye on the height and spread; it's easy for them to creep up in size.

7 Once you have three beautiful, delicate and balanced designs, add the last tweaks of texture to bring it all to a finale. Carefully place a few fine grass stems to stick above the rest of the plants and add that extra bit of detail to catch the eye.

TIPS

- Multiply these amounts to scale up for an event or wedding.
- Personalize this design by adapting it to your own flower selection or colour palette.
- These make stunning, one-of-a-kind gifts.

Resources

I'm always on the lookout for interesting suppliers of flowers, seeds, tools and materials. Making connections between other heartfelt businesses can bring extra joy to the whole making process. There's nothing better than discovering likeminded, passionate flower growers and seed producers who have just the things you're looking for. Here are a few great suppliers to get you started with a some of the things you'll need, but do explore who your local suppliers might be, too.

Flowers

AMBLE & TWINE, AUS
Gorgeous Australian flowers and seeds grown in New South Wales.
ambleandtwine.com

ATLAS FLOWERS, UK
A wholesale supplier of a large range of dried flowers and florist's sundries.
atlasflowers.co.uk

CHARLES LITTLE & COMPANY, USA
A lovely selection of farm-grown dried flowers.
charleslittleandcompany.com

LAMBOO DRIED & DECO, NL
A great range of everlasting flowers Grown on their farm in the Netherlands
lamboodrieddeco.com

LSF WHOLESALE, UK
A wholesale supplier of UK grown and imported everlasting flowers.
lsfwholesale.co.uk

RAVENSHILL FLOWER FARM, UK
A small-scale flower farm using organic, wildlife-friendly growing methods.
ravenshillflowerfarm.co.uk

WILD AT HEART – CHARLIE ARMOUR, UK
A beautiful range of small-scale, lovingly grown dried flowers.
wildatheartcharliearmour.com

Seeds

ALMA PROUST, UK
Lovely seeds with an increasing catalogue.
milliproust.com

BLACK SHED FLOWERS, UK
A brilliant selection of interesting seeds.
blackshed.flowers

CHILTERN SEEDS, UK
A great range of flower seeds, with new ones added each year.
chilternseeds.co.uk

PLANTS OF DISTINCTION SEEDS, UK
I have been buying these seeds for many years. A good selection of seeds that is growing all the time.
plantsofdistinction.co.uk

Tools and materials

AGRA-WOOL, NL
Compostable floral foam. I would not advise the use of conventional floral foam made from toxic materials that do not biodegrade.
agra-wool.nl

BARNEL, USA
Barnel make my preferred type of floristry scissors.
barnel.com

JAMES BURNETT-STUART POTTERY, UK
The stunning handmade pottery pots, jugs, vases and bowls used throughout this book are made by James Burnett-Stuart.
jamesburnettstuart.co.uk

LBS HORTICULTURE, UK
This is where I buy most of my tools from.
lbsbuyersguide.co.uk

THE MESH COMPANY, UK
I buy my chicken wire from my local farm supplies store, but many garden centres will sell it too. It's even better if you can find some old chicken-wire fencing to re-use. Alternatively, the Mesh Company sells all sorts of mesh.
themeshcompany.com

NIWAKI, UK
Floristry scissors and secateurs.
niwaki.com

NORTHERN HANDS, UK
A beautiful length of fluttering silk ribbon hand dyed using plants and flowers is the ultimate garnish to set off beautiful flowers. Northern Hands has a glorious selection of hand-dyed colours and textures for all occasions.
northern-hands-uk.com

PHOAM LABS, UK
Environmentally friendly, compostable floral foam.
phoamlabs.com

SOMERSET WILLOW GROWERS, UK
I normally forage my own willow rods for flower-panel frame making, but there are many great willow growers around if foraging isn't for you.
willowgrowers.co.uk

TRIANGLE NURSERY, UK
For wire, twine and all other floristry tools and materials, most good floristry suppliers will have a sundries section, including Triangle Nursery.
trianglenursery.co.uk

Index

Thanks

Thank you to the team at Greenfinch for being so supportive, encouraging and positive throughout the entire process. Thank you to the editorial director, Emily, and project editor, Victoria, for seeking me out, believing in me from the start and making this process such a pleasure. And to the designer, Sarah, for working with us to make this book look beautiful, and for your patience with and inclusiveness of our ideas. We appreciate it.

To all my wonderful friends and family who have been cheering me on, listening to me going on about little else and putting up with me cancelling nearly every social engagement for the last few months, you are all totally wonderful and I love and appreciate you all very much. A special thanks to Clare and Finn for letting me use their fireplace to decorate, and for providing much-needed photography lighting on a very dull day, and to Jenny for her great interior photo on page 32.

But most of all, the biggest, most heartfelt thank you to my amazing husband Rob, who agreed to take on the role of photographer while I put together the projects in these pages (having only ever picked up a camera under guidance for the odd picture of me over the years). You took on the challenge and have mastered it, remaining calm (mostly) even when I didn't explain things very well or got frustrated. It has been such a lovely thing to spend time working on this together. I will miss it. I am so proud of how well you've done. Not only that, but you have also taken on proofreading my manuscript and responding to a lot of my emails, while at the same time cheering me on, being my creative sounding board and doing the lion's share of the school runs. I really could not have done this without you by my side; I am so grateful to have you as co-creator of this book. You are now a pro photographer without ever meaning to be!

To my three beautiful girls, Tilly, Goldie and Merry, your cuddles at the end of each day have kept me going. Your humour and unwavering support in this – even though it's cut short many things we would normally have done – has meant the world to me. I am a very lucky mum to have such kind, thoughtful, supportive girls like you. I love you all so, so much.

Last but not least, to everyone who has taken an interest in my work over the years – the customers who have bought my flowers, the workshop attendees, the internet connections and friendships made, and those asking when I would be writing a book – thank you. Thank you for your part in helping me to get to this point. You have fed my creativity over the years and given it purpose. I am so grateful for you all.

First published in Great Britain in 2025 by

Greenfinch
An imprint of Quercus Editions Limited
Carmelite House
50 Victoria Embankment
London EC4Y 0DZ

An Hachette UK company

The authorized representative in the EEA is Hachette Ireland, 8 Castlecourt Centre, Castleknock Road, Castleknock, Dublin 15, D15 YF6A, Ireland

A CIP catalogue record for this book is available from the British Library

HB ISBN 978-1-52944-057-7

10 9 8 7 6 5 4 3 2 1

Designer Sarah Pyke
Project Editor Victoria Lympus
Editorial Director Emily Arbis

Printed and bound in China by C&C Offset Printing Co., Ltd.

Papers used by Greenfinch are from well-managed forests and other responsible sources.